CAMP
COOKING

OVER 100 RECIPES

by THE NATIONAL MUSEUM
of FOREST SERVICE HISTORY

Gibbs Smith

Second Edition

28 27 26 25 24   5 4 3 2 1

First Gibbs Smith edition published in 2004.
Second Gibbs Smith edition published July 2024.

Published by
Gibbs Smith, Publisher
570 N. Sportsplex Dr.
Kaysville, Utah 84037

1.800.835.4993 orders
www.gibbs-smith.com

Designed by Sheryl Dickert
Image Credits:
Cover illustration by Aisyahnada/Shutterstock.com
Endpaper pattern by JenAs/Shutterstock.com
Chapter opener illustration by sivvector/Shutterstock.com
Camping icons by Farik gallery/Shutterstock.com and Vasya Kobelev/Shutterstock.com
Bear icons by M.Style/Shutterstock.com

The Library of Congress has cataloged the first edition as follows:

Camp cooking : 100 years, 1905-2005 / a "New Century of Service" project from
the Intermountain Region and the National Museum of Forest Service History.
        p. cm.
     At head of title: USDA Forest Service.
     Includes index.
     ISBN-13:978-1-58685-761-5 (first edition) ISBN-10:1-58685-761-4 (first edition)
     1. Outdoor cookery. 2. Backpacking. 3. United States. Forest Service. I. National Museum of Forest
Service History. II. United States. Forest Service. Intermountain Region. III. United States. Forest Service.
TX823.C26 2005
641.5'78—dc22

ISBN: 978-1-4236-6760-5
Ebook ISBN: 978-1-4236-1222-3

Printed and bound in China
This product is made of FSC®-certified and other controlled material.

MIX
Paper | Supporting
responsible forestry
FSC® C144853

Contents

ACKNOWLEDGMENTS 5

FOREWORD 6

DUTCH OVEN BASICS 7

BREAKFAST 9

BREADS 25

VEGETABLES 45

SIDE DISHES 69

MAIN DISHES... 75

DESSERTS 155

RECIPE INDEX 186

REGIONS OF THE USDA FOREST SERVICE 190

ABOUT THE AUTHOR.....................................192

Acknowledgments

In researching volumes of historical documents, diaries, oral histories, letters from retirees, and published memories, we found scattered bits of information pertaining to early-day subsistence by our U.S. Forest Service predecessors. With the rough-and-tumble culture of the early ranger, cooking and eating were daily necessities that were not formally documented. They are captured instead in anecdotes and historical photographs, several of which have been selected from U.S. Forest Service archives and included in this cookbook. Photos from other sources are noted in captions.

The recipes are from U.S. Forest Service employees, retirees, and friends. Readers will find that all recipes can be used with modern outdoor-cooking methods and ingredients.

Special thanks goes to Dian Thomas, daughter of former Forest Ranger Julian Thomas from the Intermountain Region. Dian gave us permission to use many of her hints, tips, and favorite Dutch oven recipes.

We would like to express our heartfelt thanks to the Heritage Cookbook Committee for their hard work and loyal support. Committee members are: Richa Wilson, Jeannette Hartog, Janet Thorsted, Pat Gardiner, Glenna Prevedel, Diane Hadley, Norma Shupla, and Lorrie Wiggins; Beth King, Editor; and Susan McDaniel, typesetting, layout, and design (first edition).

BITTERROOT FLATS CAMPGROUND ON ROCK CREEK, LOLO NATIONAL FOREST, MONTANA, 1932 OR 1933. (PHOTO BY K. D. SWAN)

Foreword

This Heritage Cookbook pays tribute to the decades of dedication given by U.S. Forest Service employees throughout the past century.

In the Northern Region's *Early Days in the Forest Service,* Volume I, the words of Joe B. Halm seem to state clearly how it was in the beginning. Halm's career began in 1909 working for Ranger Edward Pulaski on a survey crew at Wallace, Idaho. He said:

"In thinking back over those early years of the Service I am impressed by the unselfish loyalty of everyone, the enthusiasm with which they worked and sweat [sic], carrying their food and beds on their backs, traveling the dim forest trails mostly without horses. Pride and loyalty to the Service and their chief carried them on, rain or shine, day after day, sleeping under the stars or in winter in soggy, leaky cabins with sagging roofs ten feet beneath the snow. That loyalty and enthusiasm has never waned, in my case at least.

"There is a bond which holds those of us remaining who traveled the forests together in those earlier days, who ate from the same pan and slept under the same blanket or snowshoed with hundred-pound packs for days, wet to the bone, sleeping by a fire on a bleak mountaintop burrowed in the snow many feet above ground. When the snow was soft we sank to our knees, staggering along under our packs, breaking trail. When the snow was crusted on steep ascents, we painfully cut steps in the treacherous icy slopes, but when the snow was firm and the going was good, we laughed, joked, and sang.

"We have all shared the dangers, too, toiling beneath those great white billows of smoke miles high, adding our mite of strength to control the fire demon and stop the destruction that those to follow may profit by and enjoy our great national heritage.

"I am sure not one regrets a single hardship, firm in the belief that each mile traveled, each step taken, has added a bit in making the Forest Service what it is today."

Dutch Oven Basics

Food that requires baking, such as biscuits, breads, and cakes, needs most of the heat on the top. Coals should be placed under the oven and on the lid at a 1 to 3 ratio with more on the lid. For roasting, the heat should be equal with the same number of coals on top as underneath. For frying, boiling, simmering, and stewing, heat should come from the bottom only. To keep biscuits and other baked food from burning on the bottom, remove the bottom heat after two-thirds of the total cooking time.

To share heat and serve dishes that are similar in cooking time, ovens can be stacked. This technique requires careful watching, however, to ensure that the bottom oven does not overcook.

Depending on the size of the Dutch oven, each briquette adds between 10 and 20 degrees of heat. Placement of briquettes is also important, because heat is more evenly distributed if placed in a circular pattern on the bottom and in checkerboard fashion on the lid. Remember that it is much easier to raise the heat in a cast-iron oven than to lower the temperature. Also, temperatures inside the oven will vary according to altitude so the cook may want to use a thermometer to check oven temperatures when using for the first few times. Rotating the oven every ten minutes will also help distribute the heat in a more uniform way. The lid can also be rotated a third of a turn in the opposite direction every ten minutes.

Pay close attention to the manufacturer's instructions for help on seasoning and curing a new cast-iron Dutch oven as well as caring for your oven after using it for the first time. Never use soap because the porous nature of the cast iron will trap the soap taste for future meals. Ovens can crack if heated too quickly or if cold liquid is poured into a very hot oven. With proper care, your cast-iron cookware will last for many years.

RON AND KAREN ASHLEY, REGION 4, RETIREES

BASIC BRIQUETTE TEMPERATURE CONTROL GUIDELINES		
Oven Size	Number of Briquettes on Top	Number of Briquettes on Bottom
10-inch	10 to 12	8 to 10
12-inch	12 to 14	10 to 12
14-inch	14 to 16	12 to 14
16-inch	16 to 18	14 to 16

BREAKFAST

BREAKFAST MEMORIES

Sausage
5 to 6 potatoes, cubed
½ small onion, chopped
¼ cup green pepper, chopped
6 to 7 eggs
Milk (optional)
¼ cup American or cheddar cheese

GRAVY:
2 tablespoons flour
Salt and pepper
1 glass milk

Cook sausage in a skillet. Remove sausage and add potatoes to skillet with grease from sausage (add shortening if needed to keep potatoes from sticking). Add onion and green pepper. Cook until potatoes are tender. Add eggs and crumbled sausage. Can add a little milk to eggs to make them fluffy. Add cheese. Cook until eggs are done.

GRAVY: Mix flour with salt and pepper in just enough grease to coat the bottom of the skillet. Brown to desired doneness and add about a glass of milk. If not enough, add water until your skillet is about ¾ full. Stir constantly until gravy starts to thicken. Remove from heat and stir until desired consistency is obtained.

NOTE: I add garlic to the potatoes as they are cooking—just enough to taste, and this works in two ways: adds a good flavor and helps keep the insects away.

SHARON WAID, REGION 8, OZARK-ST. FRANCIS NATIONAL FORESTS, ARKANSAS, RETIREE

DUTCH OVEN BREAKFAST

2 tablespoons olive oil
2 cloves garlic, crushed
1 Polish kielbasa sausage

2 onions, sliced
4 potatoes, boiled and chopped
1 tablespoon diced green chiles

In a 10-inch Dutch oven, heat olive oil, add garlic. Stir twice and add sausage. Brown on both sides. Add onions, cook until tender. Add potatoes and chiles and simmer 10 minutes.

HUGH AND PAM THOMPSON, REGION 4, RETIREES

STUFFED FRENCH TOAST

Texas toast
Cream cheese
Eggs
Milk

Salt
Cinnamon
Syrup
Powdered sugar

Chunk bread and cream cheese in a bowl. Mix in eggs, milk, salt, cinnamon, and syrup and let sit overnight in the refrigerator. Place in a Dutch oven and bake until done. Serve with powdered sugar and/or syrup.

DAN KRUTINA, REGION 4, RETIREE

TIP

A pinch of baking soda stirred into milk that is to be boiled will keep it from curdling.

FOREST SERVICE RECONNAISSANCE PARTY IN CAMP AT LAKE ABUNDANCE. RANGER CARL S. WALKER STANDING, DAVE MACLAY SEATED IN BACK OF STOVEPIPE, SUPERVISOR DERRICK WITHOUT HAT, PERCY MELIS BACK VIEW SECOND TO LEFT, ABSAROKA NATIONAL FOREST, MONTANA, JULY 1938. (PHOTO BY K. D. SWAN)

COWBOY BREAKFAST

1 roll sausage; bacon and ham can be added
½ cup chopped onion
1 dozen eggs
¼ cup milk or 2 tablespoons sour cream
Salt and pepper
4 to 6 slices Velveeta cheese

Cook sausage, bacon, ham, and onion. Beat eggs and milk or sour cream.
Pour mixture over meats and onion. Cook in large skillet over open
fire. Add salt and pepper to taste. Top with cheese. Optional: chopped
hashbrown potatoes, mushrooms, and bell peppers can be added.

JUDY BOREN, REGION 8, LAND BETWEEN THE LAKES
NATIONAL RECREATION AREA, KENTUCKY

SCOUTS COOKING SUPPER AT SCOUT LAKE CAMP, WASATCH NATIONAL
FOREST, UTAH, AUGUST 1935. (PHOTO BY K. D. SWAN)

HUNGRY MAN BREAKFAST

1 pound bacon
2 medium onions, diced
2 cans mushrooms, drained
1 green pepper, diced
3 cloves garlic, minced

10 to 12 medium potatoes, sliced
Salt and pepper to taste
1 dozen eggs, beaten
2 cups grated cheddar cheese
Salsa or barbecue sauce (optional)

Heat 12-inch Dutch oven until hot, using 18 to 20 briquettes on the bottom. Cut bacon into 1-inch slices and fry till brown. Add onions, mushrooms, green pepper, and garlic and sauté until onions are translucent. Add potatoes and season with salt and pepper. Cover and bake using 8 briquettes on the bottom and 14 to 16 on top for 30 minutes. Season eggs with salt and pepper, then pour over top of potatoes. Cover and bake another 20 minutes. Stir every 5 minutes. When eggs are done, cover top with cheese and replace lid. Let stand until cheese is melted. Serves 10 to 12. Can use salsa or barbecue sauce to top.

Bob VanGieson, Region I, retiree

FIELD NOTE

Former Regional Forester CLARENCE N. WOODS paid tribute to old-timers on occasion of the 50th anniversary at a family meeting in Ogden, Utah. He said, "50 years ago we didn't travel deluxe. Occasionally we swam our horses across a stream at flood stage. We made trips of several days on skis, with backpacks, no bedding, camping out where night found us, or sleeping awhile during the day in the sun and skiing part of the night, sometimes in temperatures near 50 degrees below zero. I commend the boys of the old brigade for their hardihood. I pay respect to the memory of those who have gone before us."

Old Timers News, *Intermountain Region, February* 1955

GIFFORD PINCHOT CAMPING IN THE ADIRONDACKS, NEW YORK, USDA FOREST SERVICE, GREY TOWERS NATIONAL HISTORIC SITE.

CAMPER'S OMELET

½ pound bacon
2 to 3 medium potatoes, unpeeled and chopped
1 medium onion, chopped
½ bell pepper, chopped
6 eggs (whisked fluffy)

1 firm tomato (optional), sliced
8 ounces sharp cheddar cheese, grated or chopped fine
Bacon, cooked and crumbled for topping

Fry bacon till crisp in cast-iron skillet. Remove bacon and fry chopped potatoes in grease until tender; throw in onion and pepper. When onion appears cooked, reduce heat to pan by moving to side of firepit or turning down the camp stove burner. Pour in eggs and cover for 3–5 minutes, stirring occasionally to avoid scorching. Place tomato slices, cheese, and crumbled bacon on top. Cover again for a few minutes until cheese melts and the tomatoes are smiling.

Remove from fire, slice in wedges, and serve. (I use a little hot sauce to kick it up a notch.) Serves 4.

JIM HASBROUCK, REGION 8, REGIONAL OFFICE, GEORGIA, RETIREE

SPORTSMAN'S BREAKFAST

6 to 8 slices bacon
8 to 10 medium unpeeled
   potatoes, washed and sliced
½ can green chiles, chopped

1 medium red onion, diced
6 eggs
Sliced cheddar cheese

Cut bacon into 1-inch pieces and place in cast-iron skillet with moderate fire. When bacon is about ¾ cooked, place potatoes and chiles in skillet and cover with a lid. When potatoes are ¾ cooked, add onions. Cook until onions are done. Add eggs and cook till eggs are done. Place slices of cheddar cheese over top before meal is served. Feeds 4 adults.

PAUL SHIELDS, REGION 4, RETIREE

TIP

Carry fresh eggs by breaking them into a tall, narrow olive-type jar. They will pour out, one at a time.

TRAILER USE IN CAMPGROUND, MEDICINE BOW NATIONAL FOREST, WYOMING, 1937. (PHOTO BY JOHN W. SPENCER)

ONE-EYED BUFFALOES

10 eggs
1½ cups milk
1 teaspoon nutmeg
1 teaspoon cinnamon

1 teaspoon vanilla
1 tablespoon oil
1 loaf bread, sliced
1 dozen or more eggs

Mix eggs, milk, nutmeg, cinnamon, and vanilla and beat well. Heat oil on griddle over fire. Dip each slice of bread into egg mixture and put on griddle. Cut out about a 3-inch circle in the bread. Break an additional egg into center of each piece of bread on griddle and fry. When bottom of toast is brown, flip over and brown top side of toast and egg. Serve one-eyed buffaloes hot with syrup, jam, or honey.

DON DUFF, REGION 4, RETIREE

FIELD NOTE

BILL MACE recalled early days in the Service as a member of the Arizona's Kaibab National Forest Reconnaissance Crew of January 1910. Crew member Nils Eckbo brought along the first pair of skis Mace had ever seen and he said, "Being a native Norwegian, Eckbo surely knew how to use them."

Mace also told of a meeting of the Kaibab and Dixie Rangers at St. George, Utah, in March of 1911. He said, "I can't remember whether I learned much about Forest Service procedure, but I shall never forget the farewell party at the close of the meeting. Dixie Rangers Alex MacFarlane and Willard Sorenson had cached a 5-gallon demijohn of Dixie wine at a convenient spot near the dance hall, which added some hilarity to the pleasure of the evening."

OLD TIMERS NEWS, INTERMOUNTAIN REGION, NOVEMBER 1955

GREEN RIVER CHILE CON QUESO OMELET

1 dozen eggs
2 (7-ounce) cans whole green chiles
½ pound cheddar cheese, sliced
2 (4-ounce) cans mushrooms (or ½ pound diced)
1 medium onion, diced
½ teaspoon cayenne pepper
½ cup milk

Combine, mix, and beat all ingredients into one mess in a bowl, pan, or whatever you have. Heat griddle over fire coals; spread mixture on griddle and divide into 4 servings. Fold over and continue cooking until done or slightly browned. Serve with chile salsa.

DON DUFF, REGION 4, RETIREE

PICNICKING AT VERMILLION CASTLE CAMPGROUND, DIXIE NATIONAL FOREST, UTAH. LOG TABLES MADE BY ERA CREWS, 1937. (PHOTO BY B. BETENSON)

HUNTING CAMP SCRAMBLED EGGS

1 teaspoon butter
Handful of diced ham, salami,
    summer sausage, or 5 to 6 slices
    bacon (cooked and crumbled)
½ can (small) green chiles, chopped
1 tomato, chopped
½ medium red onion, chopped
3 to 4 green onions, chopped

3 to 4 fresh mushrooms, sliced
½ cup alfalfa sprouts
1 to 2 fresh jalapeño
    peppers, chopped
6 eggs, beaten with ¼ cup milk
Black pepper, coarse ground
Seasoned salt
¼ cup cheddar cheese, diced

Place teaspoon of butter in frying pan and heat at medium temperature. Place all ingredients except eggs, seasonings, and cheese in pan and cook until onions and tomato are nearly done. Add eggs, stirring occasionally, and cook until almost done. Add seasonings and cheese. Remove from heat as soon as cheese begins to melt and eggs are done. Feeds 4 adults.

PAUL SHIELDS, REGION 4, RETIREE

GIRLS TRYING TO AVOID SMOKE FROM GRILL MADE FROM 55-GALLON DRUM WITH GRATE, CACHE NATIONAL FOREST, UTAH, CIRCA 1950.

FIELD NOTE ▶ Following is the story of how a chance visit to a church in Cody, Wyoming, changed the entire life of a young man in 1904.

"I was seated beside a sturdy, pleasant young fellow about my own age. We exchanged the usual few words as strangers might. He introduced himself as Clarence N. Woods. I replied that my name was Clarence also, but Clarence B. Swim. This, of course, was before the services had gotten underway. Woods asked me if I was employed. I told him that I did not have steady work. He told me that he was a ranger on the Shoshone Forest Reserve, and for me to call at the Supervisor's office the following morning and that he might be able to arrange for me to start work. I called at the office; Woods was the only person present. After the usual questions of qualifications, health, etc., he told me that with approval of the Supervisor he felt sure that he could start me in on Forest Service work as Forest Guard at $60 per month, pending final approval and appointment from the Washington Office. . . . . My temporary appointment took place early May of 1904. I was given a lineup of the equipment I would need to start out with—a couple of horses, a riding and pack saddle, bedding, a tarp or tent, an axe and shovel, cooking outfit, a gun, and grub for at least a couple of weeks. My bank account was already low, but I made the best of it and started out on this new adventure. I bought a little black nag, with black eyes, for a saddle horse, for $50. I bought a glass-eyed Indian pony with ring bones for a pack horse. I bought a Collins and Morrison saddle for $56, and pack saddle equipment. Next was bedding. For a greenhorn I did pretty well. I bought a .25-35 Winchester rifle and a .38 Colt that one couldn't hit the broad side of a barn with. I later traded this worthless Colt in on a Luger pistol, an excellent, accurate gun. Next on the list was grub. I bought bacon, ham, flour, baking powder, beans, canned fruit, dried prunes, and a box of loaf sugar. Woods spent the evening with me giving final instructions and teaching me the art of packing and throwing the diamond hitch."

EARLY DAYS IN THE FOREST SERVICE, VOLUME I, NORTHERN REGION

HUNTER'S SPECIAL SAUSAGE BREAKFAST DUTCH OVEN FEAST

12 to 15 slices bread, cubed
1 cube butter, melted
1 pound grated cheddar cheese
18 eggs

¾ cup milk
1 teaspoon dry mustard
Salt and pepper to taste
1 pound cooked sausage

Add bread cubes to a well-greased 12-inch Dutch oven. Drizzle butter over bread then sprinkle with the grated cheese. Whisk together eggs, milk, and mustard in a bowl. Add salt and pepper to your liking. Pour eggs over bread and cheese. Sprinkle the cooked sausage on the top. Cover and bake using 6 to 8 briquettes on the bottom and 12 to 14 briquettes for the top for 30–45 minutes, or until eggs are set. Serves 8 to 10 people.

JOHN HOEL, REGION 4, REGIONAL OFFICE, RETIREE

RANGER JACK MCNUTT VISITS WITH PICNICKERS ON MOUNTAIN MAHOGANY GROVE, NEVADA NATIONAL FOREST, JUNE 1940. (PHOTO BY P. S. BIELER)

HUEVOS TIXIEROS

2 packages precooked
   breakfast sausages
Garlic salt
1 dozen eggs
½ can chopped green chiles
½ bell pepper, chopped

¼ cup chopped onion
⅓ cup milk
6 Waverly crackers
Black pepper
Salsa

Cut sausages into ¼-inch cartwheels, brown in large cast-iron skillet over medium fire, drain excess grease, sprinkle with garlic salt. In small bowl mix eggs, green chiles, bell pepper, onion, milk, and crushed crackers. Pour egg mixture in skillet and add pepper; let set up and then stir minimum amount until done. Serve with salsa, biscuits, and honey. Serves about 4 (hungry) or 6 (not very).

Stan Tixier, Region 4, retiree

TIP

BATTERIES AND STEEL WOOL FIRE STARTER

An easy and dramatic way to start a fire is to use two flashlight batteries and a strip of grade 00 or finer steel wool. Cut or stretch a piece of steel wool—about 8 inches in length. Align two good flashlight batteries on top of each other in an upright position (as if they were placed inside a flashlight). Hold one end of the steel wool strip against the bottom of the lower battery. Carefully rub the other end of the steel wool across the "nub" of the upper battery. As soon as the steel wool sparks, place it on tinder or other burnable material and slowly blow on it. As you blow, the flame will grow more intense. This method works very well for starting a fire in windy areas. For safety reasons, always pack the steel wool and batteries in separate containers.

Dian Thomas, from Recipes for Roughing It Easy

FIELD NOTE WILLIAM W. MORRIS, who worked on the Coeur d'Alene National Forest in Idaho from 1909 to 1914, wrote about his experiences with rough reconnaissance work.

He wrote, "Most of the summer we spent in a little tent or sometimes in the open. The country was new and almost unexplored. Occasionally we would come to an old settler's cabin, and sleeping in one of these one night, I had my first experience with pack rats. The pack rat is a large mountain rat, so named because it has the habit of packing off to its nest almost everything that it sees. They seem to be particularly partial to all bright shiny objects, such as spoons, silver dollars, etc. The woodsmen regard them with more or less superstition, as they have a peculiar method of tapping in the nighttime, when one is trying to sleep, much in the manner of the Morse telegraph code. This they do with their back feet. I remember one old cabin where we slept one night; a carpet had been hung out at the head of a bed built of logs. When we laid down in the bed our heads touched against this carpet. I remember waking up several times in the night, feeling a pack rat rubbing against my head, as it ran back and forth on the other side of the carpet. There had been some volunteer potatoes come up near this cabin, and that night the pack rats had been working diligently, and had cut all these potato stalks down and placed them all in front of our cabin door where we saw them the first thing in the morning on going to make our ablutions in the cold mountain stream flowing near. My friend the cruiser remarked that he thought it was a 'whitecap' warning to get out, which we did, as our work at this place was completed."

EARLY DAYS IN THE FOREST SERVICE, *VOLUME I, NORTHERN REGION*

RIVER RUNNIN' COFFEE

Use coffee pot or empty 1-pound coffee tin. Fill tin with water to within 1 inch of top of tin. Holds 12 cups of water. Put in 1 tablespoon of coffee for each cup. Set tin on red-hot bed of coals and forget about it until it boils. Take pot off coals and add ½ cup cold water to settle grounds, or toss in two eggshells to do the same thing.

To clean inside of tin, wipe dry with paper towels or cloth. Use no soap! To reduce soot on outside of tin, coat outside of tin with soap before putting it on coals. Soot will then wash off, even in cold water.

Don Duff, Region 4, retiree

Cornelia and Gifford Pinchot over campfire, USDA Forest Service, Grey Towers National Historic Site.

QUICK SCONES

1 cup vegetable oil for frying
4 to 6 English muffins, cut in half
2 to 3 cups prepared pancake batter
Toppings of your choice

Heat a 12-inch Dutch oven over 12 to 15 hot coals. Heat oil until a drop of pancake batter dropped into the skillet sizzles. With a fork, dip muffins into the pancake batter and carefully add to the hot oil. Cook on both sides until golden brown. Remove and drain on paper towels. Serve hot with toppings, as desired. Serves 4.

Serve plain or topped with sugar, powdered sugar, brown sugar, cinnamon sugar, honey, jam, jelly, or syrup.

Dian Thomas, from Recipes for Roughing It Easy

A hearty breakfast for the river recreationists before continuing down the Salmon River, Nez Perce National Forest, Idaho, July 23, 1957. (Photo by A. W. Blackerby)

BREADS

DIAN THOMAS, author of 12 bestselling outdoor cookbooks, and daughter of Julian Thomas, long-time District Ranger of the Manti-LaSal and Wasatch-Cache National Forests, got her start cooking over open campfires as a child. Dian has been gracious enough to share some of her recipes and cooking hints for this publication. Following is the introduction written for her bestselling cookbook, *Recipes for Roughing It Easy.*

My fondness for outdoor cooking, which has always been vivid in my memory, began when I was a very young child. My father, Julian Thomas, was a forest ranger on the Manti–LaSal National Forest in the mountains of southern Utah. I loved to accompany him when he took our family to the wilderness for outings and recreation.

My first taste of outdoor cooking was my dad's homemade sourdough biscuits. Both of my grandfathers raised sheep and lived in sheepherder's wagons. My dad's outdoor cooking followed his father's example, which included baking sourdough biscuits in a Dutch oven. As the biscuits were cooking—and I'm certain they reached at least four inches in height—I remember the fragrant, heavenly scent as steam came wafting out of the oven. I would slather a hot biscuit with butter and honey. Then I would barely need to chew as the delicious biscuit melted in my mouth. I fell in love with outdoor cooking at that moment.

Some of my favorite recipes can be found on pages 24, 28, 30, 31, 38, 62, 70, 71, 77, 81, 82, 99, 120, 122, 151, 154, 162, 164, 166, 176, 178.

DIAN THOMAS, FROM RECIPES FOR ROUGHING IT EASY

SOURDOUGH BREAD

In pioneer days, sourdough was developed from a culture of flour, water, and wild yeast. Wild yeast is atmospheric bacteria, similar to that used for souring milk or making cottage cheese. The "starter" plus dough merged with ingredients to create unlimited breads and biscuits. One or two cups of starter always remains to activate new dough; that's why it is called the "starter." Today, it's easy to make a starter with flour, sugar, yeast, and water.

ABOUT CONTAINERS

The most common sourdough container for camp or home use is a 1- to 2-gallon earthenware crock with a loose-fitting lid. Plastic or glass containers with loose-fitting lids or plastic wrap work equally well. Acids from the bacterial action of the dough react on metal; thus metal containers are not recommended. It is essential that the lid or cover be loose or unsealed because the contents might explode if gas cannot expand and escape.

*DIAN THOMAS,
FROM RECIPES FOR
ROUGHING IT EASY*

*JULIAN THOMAS AND HIS
FAVORITE DUTCH OVENS.*

MAKING SOURDOUGH STARTER

Your homemade starter will work just as well as one that has been passed down through generations. Some families pride themselves on its length of time in use, and many even give their starter a name.

1 cup all-purpose flour
½ tablespoon dry yeast

1 teaspoon sugar
1½ cups warm water

In a crock or plastic container, combine flour, yeast, and sugar, then add warm water. Leave at room temperature for 3 days, adding 1 cup additional flour and ½ cup warm water each day until batter is active—odor is pungent and the surface is bubbly. This occurs from the gas released by the action of the yeast. At this point your starter is ready to form the basis of sourdough recipes. Remember to set aside 1 to 2 cups of starter for the next batch. The amount of dough you mix will depend on the number of bread loaves or biscuits desired.

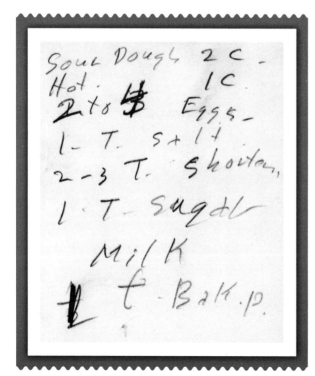

JULIAN THOMAS'
ORIGINAL
HANDWRITTEN
SOURDOUGH
RECIPE CARD.
(DIAN THOMAS,
RECIPES FOR
ROUGHING IT
EASY)

MAINTAINING SOURDOUGH STARTER

To maintain the starter, use the dough frequently. The starter will keep for several days and even weeks by refrigerating or freezing between uses. When making a new batch of bread or pancakes, bring the starter to room temperature a day or so before using and let it reactivate at a warm (not hot) temperature.

To shorten rising time, mix the dough with warm water and keep it in a warm place. To lengthen rising time, mix the dough with cold water and keep it in a cool place until you plan to use it.

In outdoor camping areas during cold periods, the dough can be mixed with warm water and covered with insulation such as coats or bedding to "wake it up." During warm weather, mix it with cold water and store in a cool place so it will not become too active.

When the dough becomes more sour, it will not make a good finished product and should be discarded, except for a small amount to activate a new starter. Adding cultured yeast helps to renew the starter. When you begin to mix the dough, the bowl should be less than half full because it will more than double in size and may overflow the container.

MIXING BREAD AND BISCUITS

The night before or several hours prior to making bread or biscuits, add 1 cup flour and ½ cup of warm water to the starter. Sourdough bread dough should be stiffer, left to rise longer, and baked longer than dough for biscuits.

The old-timers who were "packing" carried flour in a seamless or heavy flour sack and rolled the top down to the level of the flour, shaped the flour with their fingers into a bowl, poured starter into the bowl, and mixed it. Today, the traditional method for making sourdough is to place flour in a deep kettle or mixing bowl and, with the backs of the fingers, mold it into a bowl shape. Into this "well" pour the desired amount of activated sourdough "starter."

DIAN THOMAS, FROM RECIPES FOR ROUGHING IT EASY

SOURDOUGH BREADS AND BISCUITS

Sourdough biscuits were a mainstay for many sheepherders. They may well become a mainstay for you too. The smell and the taste are incredible.

All-purpose flour to cover the bottom of a kettle or bowl
2 cups sourdough starter
1 teaspoon salt
1 teaspoon baking powder
¼ teaspoon baking soda
¼ cup shortening or bacon drippings, melted
2 tablespoons sugar

Combine flour, sourdough starter, salt, baking powder, baking soda, shortening or drippings, and sugar, using the "well" method described on page 29.

Knead thoroughly by folding from the outside to the center using your hands or a spoon. Make bread dough stiffer than biscuit dough. Shape into loaves, oblong or round, or biscuits. Ease dough for bread into a buttered loaf or round heatproof bowl or an oiled 12-inch Dutch oven. For biscuits, shape into small balls in your hand and place them side by side into a buttered or oiled 12-inch Dutch oven or cake pan. Brush the top with oil. Let them rise, covered with plastic wrap, until doubled in size.

DUTCH OVEN AND AT HOME

Heat Dutch oven using 10 hot coals on the bottom. Cover with a Dutch oven lid and place 14 hot coals on top. Bake:

Bread loaf about 1 hour (350 degrees)
Biscuits 20–30 minutes (350 degrees)

DIAN THOMAS, FROM RECIPES FOR ROUGHING IT EASY

SOURDOUGH PANCAKES

An essential to making good pancakes is cooking them on a hot griddle.
The griddle should smoke when greased or oiled, and it should sizzle
if water is dropped onto it. Make a small sample cake to see if it turns
golden brown instead of light brown or "whitish." A griddle that is not
hot enough will not make good cakes; if it is too hot, cakes will burn. A
heavy aluminum or iron griddle, a Dutch oven, or a Dutch oven lid will
give pleasing results.

1 cup sourdough starter	3 tablespoons oil
1 cup prepared dry pancake mix	1 tablespoon sugar
2 eggs	

In a medium mixing bowl, blend sourdough starter, dry pancake mix,
eggs, oil, and sugar. Do not over-stir. If batter is too thick, thin with milk.
Add ¼ teaspoon baking soda if the dough is too sour. Ladle onto a hot
griddle. Turn over when light brown.

Serve pancakes warm from the griddle. The quality diminishes if they are
stacked or allowed to rest and cool. Makes 10 to 12.

DIAN THOMAS, FROM RECIPES FOR ROUGHING IT EASY

CAMP STOVE, WASATCH
NATIONAL FOREST,
UTAH, CIRCA 1935.

DUTCH OVEN BASQUE SHEEPHERDER'S BREAD

1 cup very hot water
½ cup butter
⅓ cup sugar
2½ teaspoons salt

2 packages dry yeast
9 to 9½ cups flour
Salad oil

In large bowl, combine hot water, butter, sugar, and salt. Stir until butter is melted. Let cool and stir in yeast. Cover and set in warm place about 15 minutes.

Beat in 5 cups flour to make thick batter. Stir in about 3½ cups more flour to make stiff dough. Turn dough onto floured board; knead until smooth and satiny, adding flour as needed to prevent sticking. Place in greased bowl; turn over to grease top. Cover and let rise until doubled. Punch dough down and knead briefly to release air; shape into smooth ball. With a circle of foil, cover the inside bottom of a 5-quart Dutch oven. Grease foil, inside of Dutch oven, and underside of lid with salad oil. Bake at 375 degrees for 30–35 minutes.

RON AND KAREN ASHLEY, REGION 4, RETIREES

FIELD NOTE

From the Intermountain Region *Old Timers News* of October 1967, RAYMOND D. GARVER told of helping survey and mark some 400 miles of forest boundary with cut cedar posts and tin boundary signs on the Toiyabe National Forest in Nevada. The year was 1913 and equipment was a sheep wagon and buckboard, a team of mules and a team of horses. The three Rangers were Kivett as cook, camp mover, and general helper; Cahill as stadia man; and Woolley as post getter and setter. Garver wrote, "Some days we could run 10 miles of line; other days half as much or less. Kivett said we worked too hard and made him get up and cook breakfast too early. Most of the time good nature prevailed."

SHEEPHERDER BREAD

⅓ cup sugar
4 teaspoons salt
¼ cup potato flakes*
¼ pound butter or margarine

2 ⅔ cups hot water (approx.)
2 packages yeast
8 ½ cups white flour

Mix sugar, salt, potato flakes, and butter with hot water until butter melts and temperature is right for yeast. Add yeast and let stand for 15 minutes. Add flour (flour and water ratio may differ with humidity). Knead for about 10 minutes. Let rise until double in volume. Knead again and place in an 8-inch Dutch oven. Let rise until dough touches lid. Bake at 350 degrees for 35 minutes. Remove lid and bake for 20–25 minutes. Top of loaf may be brushed with butter.

*Potato water from boiled potatoes, instead of plain water, is the traditional Basque method. The potato flakes are a convenient substitute.

JERRY DAVIS, FORMER REGION 4, HUMBOLDT-TOIYABE NATIONAL FOREST EMPLOYEE

AUTOMOBILE CAMPERS TOURING THROUGH THE PIKE NATIONAL FOREST, COLORADO, JULY 1916. (PHOTO BY W. J. HUTCHINSON)

FIELD NOTE

DEWITT RUSSELL recalled a 1924 pack trip on the Garden Valley District of the Boise National Forest that he took with his wife, Goldie, and 8-month-old baby, John.

Little John rode on a pillow on Goldie's saddle horn and all went well until the family came up against a huge Ponderosa pine tree that completely blocked their way. Worried that baby John might be injured during their detour, they left him sleeping under a tree hemmed in with rocks so that he couldn't roll out. Goldie, in the lead, got though their detour without any trouble and DeWitt's saddle horse also made it through fine. But old Finny, the pack mare, stepped in the wrong place. "Her feet flew out from under her and down she went. First she rolled, and since nothing stopped her, she bounded. The air was full of ropes, blankets, tools, and sundry other things. Rocks were rolling and dust was flying. We dropped horses and everything in order to get to the baby. As we hurried along I got a glimpse of Finny standing in the creek with nothing on but a halter and a very baffled look on her face. We found John still asleep and he had missed the entire show. As we gathered up our outfit, I was due for another shock. About the first thing I picked up was a burlap-wrapped bundle of 40 percent dynamite! The caps were rolled up in my coat behind my saddle.

"Because the horse had ended up in a large clump of alders about 18 ft. high, she was rendered useless for the rest of the season. We found old Finney was so stiff that taking her home was out of the question. We got her out of the creek onto a nice little meadow and left her there. Due to the stress of a bad fire season, I did not get back to her. She came back to the station unaided about a month later."

OLD TIMERS NEWS, *INTERMOUNTAIN REGION, JUNE 1971*

DILLY CASSEROLE BREAD

1 package yeast
¼ cup warm water
1 cup creamed cottage cheese
2 tablespoons sugar
1 tablespoon instant minced onion
1 tablespoon butter

2 teaspoons dill seed
1 teaspoon salt
¼ teaspoon baking soda
1 egg
2¼ to 2½ cups flour

Dissolve yeast in water. Heat cottage cheese to lukewarm. Combine sugar, onion, butter, dill seed, salt, baking soda, and egg in a bowl with cheese and yeast mixture. Add flour to form a stiff dough. Cover and let rise until doubled in bulk. Stir down dough. Turn into a well-greased 8-inch Dutch oven. Let rise 30–40 minutes, or until light. Bake over coals and with coals on lid, 40–50 minutes. Brush with butter and sprinkle with salt.

GEORGE AND PAT ROETHER, REGION 4, RETIREES

1941 PICNIC AT PINE VALLEY, DIXIE NATIONAL FOREST, UTAH.

DUTCH OVEN BEER BREAD

3 cups self-rising flour
1 can warm beer
3 tablespoons sugar

Mix all ingredients and place in a greased Dutch oven. Bake over hot coals about 1 hour. Place a few hot coals on lid so top of bread will brown.

LouJean Findlay, Region 4, retiree

FIELD NOTE

ROSIE WAGNER had a great reputation for turning out a big wash boiler full of raised doughnuts over a campfire as easily as he could cargo, pack, and pull a string of mules cross-country, but he wasn't one to put up with foolishness. One morning after beating on a dishpan for ten minutes, without much response from the bedded-down firefighters, he yelled, "Are you guys going to come and get it or do you want me to funnel you!"

Early Days in the Forest Service, Volume 4, Northern Region

The main fire camp for the Pueblo Canyon Fire, Cibola National Forest, New Mexico, 1939.

FIELD NOTE

JOSEPH B. HALM told of early-day hardship in 1910 logging camps in Idaho.

He wrote, "Supplies had been packed in from Cataldo, Idaho, by pack string before the heavy snows came. These supplies were brought in over the divide then up the Little North Fork through sixteen fords, which became difficult and treacherous when ice began to form and the river to gorge and rise. After the packers had made their last trip for the winter, we ate what we had: corned beef, bacon, ham, dried beans and fruit, and canned vegetables, bread, and oleomargarine.

"During the worst storms we were snowbound and spent our time reading the few worn magazines by what light filtered through the small dingy windows or played cribbage. The cards became so badly worn and dirty the spots could not be recognized. The men became restless, discontented, and irritable during these times.

"At our camp twenty-eight men lived and slept in one squat and dingy shake-roofed log cabin 16 x 28 feet wide with one door and two windows set horizontal in the two long side walls. The double bunks made of poles and filled with boughs were double-decked and extended around the entire wall space except at the windows and door. A Sibley stove occupied the center of the room and at night the tiers of wet musty socks and other garments dangled like a Monday wash from the ceiling around the stovepipe. The air was always putrid and vermin prospered in the bunks. A wooden water bucket and two basins near a window served for all the men; shaving was a luxury. What a scramble for socks in the morning, first come first served. Ours was not an exceptional camp for those days before regulations required more sanitation."

EARLY DAYS IN THE FOREST SERVICE, VOLUME I, NORTHERN REGION

SPOON BREAD

3 strips bacon, diced
2 (8-ounce) packages corn muffin mix, unprepared
2 teaspoons baking powder
1 (4-ounce) package blue cheese, crumbled (optional)
4 eggs, beaten
1½ cups milk
2 tablespoons butter or margarine, melted

Heat a 12-inch Dutch oven over 9 hot coals and sauté bacon until well cooked. Pour off all but 1 tablespoon of drippings. In a mixing bowl, add corn muffin mix, baking powder, and cheese. In a small bowl, blend eggs, milk, and butter or margarine and add to dry ingredients. Pour batter into hot drippings. Cover with Dutch oven lid with 15 hot coals on top. Bake, covered, 20–30 minutes, or until evenly browned and top springs back in the center. Serves 8 to 12.

Dian Thomas, from Recipes for Roughing It Easy

Family roasts hot dogs at a fireplace at Grizzly Bear Campground, Black Hills National Forest, South Dakota, August 1957. (Photo by Bluford W. Muir)

An old camping trick was to pack cooking utensils in wooden boxes that could later be stacked and used as shelving in tents or campgrounds. Boy Scouts also used this method of transporting their camp cooking gear and some very sophisticated boxes are now available commercially for the same use. The photos on this page show two campsites on the Toiyabe National Forest, Nevada, where these boxes were used at the Kyle Canyon Campground in 1934.

CINNAMON BISCUIT ON A STICK

1 can store-bought biscuits
1 container squeeze butter
Cinnamon/sugar shaker mixture

Roll out a biscuit with your hands so that it becomes elongated and about 1 inch thick at the center. Wrap the biscuit around a shish kabob skewer or other cleaned stick. Pinch the dough as you wrap it around the stick to ensure it stays on the stick while cooking. When done wrapping the biscuit, it should take up about 6 inches of the stick. Heat over the campfire until golden brown. Pull off the stick and drizzle with the squeeze butter, then sprinkle with cinnamon/sugar mixture.

JANET THORSTED, REGION 4, REGIONAL OFFICE, UTAH

SEYMOUR HAYDEN COOKING DOUGHNUTS FOR THE CREW AT A PRESCRIBED BURNING CAMP SET UP IN STOCKING MEADOWS ON THE CLARKIA RANGER DISTRICT, ST. JOE NATIONAL FOREST, IDAHO (NOW PART OF THE IDAHO PANHANDLE NATIONAL FORESTS), IN THE FALL OF 1968. (PHOTO BY BERT E. STROM, BOISE NATIONAL FOREST RETIREE)

CINNAMON ROLLS

DOUGH:
2 packages dry yeast
1 quart warmed milk
¼ cup lukewarm water
2 tablespoons sugar
2 eggs, beaten
2 tablespoons oil
1½ teaspoons salt
3 teaspoons baking powder
½ teaspoon baking soda
8 cups flour

FILLING:
2 cups sugar
4 teaspoons cinnamon

GLAZE:
3 sticks butter
5 cups powdered sugar
1 teaspoon vanilla
Enough milk to make creamy

Dissolve yeast in warm water; then add rest of dough ingredients and mix into a smooth, soft dough. Add enough flour until dough is no longer sticky when kneaded. Cover and let rise. Punch down and roll out to about ½ inch thick and 12 inches wide. Sprinkle with filling ingredients. Press filling into dough then roll up, seal the edges, and slice into rolls about 1 inch thick. Place into two cold Dutch ovens. Place ovens on coals and add more on the lid. For 12-inch oven, use 7 briquettes on bottom and 12 on top. After you smell the rolls baking, don't lift the lid! Check rolls about 15 minutes later. When they are done, remove from coals and let cool slightly. Mix together the glaze and spread on the rolls.

BILLY KEITH, REGION 4, RETIREE

TRICK TO COOKING ROLLS OR BISCUITS IN DUTCH OVENS

Buy a small aluminum cake pan that will fit inside your oven. Place 3 nickels in the bottom of the oven and then place the pan with the rolls on these (holds the pan up so the bottom of the rolls don't burn). Cook the rolls for 15 minutes and then check them. Don't put too many coals under the oven when cooking breads—they burn easily.

BREAKFAST CINNAMON ROLLS

This is to be prepared the night before and cooked in the morning.

24 Rhodes frozen roll dough
1 cup brown sugar
2 tablespoons cinnamon

½ cup chopped nuts
½ cup melted butter
Frosting (optional)

Line a 12-inch Dutch oven with heavy foil and spray generously with cooking spray. Cut the frozen roll dough into halves and place in oven. Sprinkle brown sugar, cinnamon, and nuts over dough. Drizzle with melted butter. Cover with lid and set aside until morning. Place over hot coals (twice as many on top as on the bottom) before the sun rises and your family and friends will awaken to hot, fresh cinnamon rolls! Drizzle with frosting for an extra sweet treat.

SUSAN MCDANIEL, REGION 4, REGIONAL OFFICE, UTAH

TOURISTS CAMPING AT GRAYBACK PUBLIC CAMPGROUND ON THE SISKIYOU NATIONAL FOREST, OREGON. (PHOTO BY TOM GILL)

LAKE FORK CAMPGROUND, IDAHO NATIONAL FOREST, AUGUST 1930. (PHOTO BY SHIPP)

STORY & SONG

RECIPE FOR A RANGER by J. B. Cammann (old-time Gunnison Ranger), quoted from the minutes of the Boise National Forest Picnic on July 1, 1956.

First get a big kettle and a fire that's hot,
And when everything's ready, throw into the pot:
A doctor, a miner, of lawyers a few,
At least one sheepherder and a cowboy or two;
Next add a surveyor, and right after that,
A man with some sense, and a good diplomat;
At least one stonemason, and then give it a stir,
And add to the mess one good carpenter.
A man that knew trees, and don't leave from the list,
A telephone man, and a fair botanist.
The next to be added is a must, that's a cinch;
It's the man that will stay when it comes to a pinch;
Add a man that will work and not stand 'round and roar,
Who can do ten thousand things and then just a few more.
Now boil it up well and skim off the scum,
And a Ranger you'll find in the residu-um.

OLD TIMERS NEWS, *INTERMOUNTAIN REGION*, OCTOBER 1981

HEATING TORTILLAS
ON AN OPEN FIRE

Tortillas are a lightweight and compact substitute for bread when camping or backpacking. They are light, easy to pack, and take up a lot less room than bread. If kept in airtight bags, they will last several days without drying out.

Either let the fire die down to just coals or spread a small amount of coals off to the side of the main fire. Lay a flour tortilla directly on these coals for 5 seconds or so, depending on how hot they are. Use your fingers or a stick to turn the tortilla over and heat the opposite side for another 5 seconds or so. Do this twice for each side. Be careful not to burn the tortilla, just heat it, although a few brown spots may be present. Remove from the coals and eat. Can be dipped in chili, beans, stew, etc., or eaten plain. The coals give a unique flavor to the tortilla.

DAN ANDERSON, REGION 4, PAYETTE NATIONAL
FOREST, MCCALL RANGER DISTRICT, IDAHO

CAMPING AT HEAD OF BIG COTTONWOOD CANYON, WASATCH NATIONAL FOREST, UTAH, 1924. (PHOTO BY F. S. BAKER)

VEGETABLES

BERT'S DUTCH OVEN DINO SPUDS

½ pound bacon, cut in
  1- to 2-inch pieces
6 to 10 brown potatoes, sliced
Lemon pepper
Powdered or diced garlic
Salt and pepper

6 to 8 ounces water
1 large yellow onion,
  sliced or chunked
1 pound cheddar or other
  cheese, sliced or shredded

Heat 24 briquettes. When gray, spread coals. Brown bacon in a 12-inch Dutch oven. Remove bacon and some of the grease. Place sliced potatoes in Dutch oven. Add lemon pepper, powdered or diced garlic, and salt and pepper to taste. Place 12 coals under oven, cover, and place 10 to 12 coals on the top. Heat about 40 minutes. After first 10 minutes, remove cover, stir, and add 6 ounces of water. Stir every 10 minutes. Add more water if needed to prevent drying. After 40 minutes stir in onions and bacon. Add more spices as needed, and spread cheese on top. Cover and cook another 10–15 minutes. Remove from heat and serve.

THIS DISH WAS USED AT THE REGION 4, REGIONAL LEADERSHIP TEAM MEETING AND THE POTLUCK AT FLAMING GORGE NATIONAL RECREATION AREA CELEBRATING DALE BOSWORTH'S SELECTION AS REGION I, REGIONAL FORESTER. I WAS SUPERVISOR OF THE ASHLEY NATIONAL FOREST AT THE TIME.

BERT KULESZA, REGION 4, REGIONAL OFFICE, UTAH, RETIREE

FIELD NOTE

BONES BALCH remembered one year on the Targhee National Forest after the dog races, when he and Lem Steele took Bill Trude's dog team to clean off some cabins in Hallie Park and Shotgun. He wrote, "Without any broken trail, the dogs could hardly pull our outfit, so I played lead dog. Going over Green Canyon Pass there was a crust, and they couldn't even hold the sleigh from backing up. I couldn't either. So I got down on all fours and I and the dogs pulled and Lem pushed until we made it. Boy, what fun in those days!"

OLD TIMERS NEWS, *INTERMOUNTAIN REGION, JUNE 1968*

PAN FRIED TATERS

Grease

8 to 10 potatoes (sliced thick and long)

1 large onion (chopped)

Salt and pepper

Place Dutch oven over open flame, heat grease until very hot. Drop in potatoes, onion, and salt and pepper. Keep potatoes turned every so often. Fry until light brown.

TERRI VINING, REGION 8, OZARK-ST. FRANCIS NATIONAL FORESTS, ARKANSAS , RETIREE

CAMPGROUND AT SHASTA LAKE, SHASTA NATIONAL FOREST, CALIFORNIA, AUGUST 1953. TOP: OTTILY BAYER, BOTTOM: MAHON BAYER: DAUGHTERS OF MR. AND MRS. OTTO BAYER, COSTA MESA, CALIFORNIA. (PHOTO BY JACK ROTTIER)

DUTCH OVEN POTATOES

1 pound bacon
6 large onions, sliced

10 pounds potatoes, sliced
Water

Fry bacon in large 14-inch Dutch oven that has been heated over cooking fire coals. Remove part of the bacon grease. Add the onions and potatoes and approximately 1 cup water. Cover and continue to cook, stirring occasionally and adding enough water to just keep moist, not soggy. Cook until vegetables are tender. These are also good with about 6 tomatoes cut up and added the last few minutes of cooking time. Also good with grated cheese added to the tomatoes.

BESSIE PERKINS, REGION 4, DIXIE NATIONAL FOREST, RETIREE

RANGERS MELLINTIN, COTTON, AND MRS. MELLINTIN MOUNTED TO MAKE THE TRIP TO A PLANTING SITE AT SAN JUAN, UTAH.

DUTCH OVEN SPUDS AND BACON

1 pound bacon, partially cooked and sliced into 1-inch strips
1 medium onion, sliced
5 pounds of Idaho red potatoes, sliced
Salt and pepper

Place a layer of bacon in the bottom of a 12-inch Dutch oven, then layer onions and spuds, and salt and pepper to taste. Repeat layering to the top. Put a little water in over the spuds, then put the lid on and place 8 briquettes under and 15 briquettes on top. Cook for 45 minutes. DO NOT OPEN AND DO NOT STIR during the 45 minutes. Open and check spuds for doneness. Smell and clear appearance of spuds will tell you they are done. At this point you can put grated cheese and sour cream on top and melt for a few minutes. (Optional, put in sliced green peppers with the onions.)

MARIAN JACKLIN, REGION 4, DIXIE NATIONAL FOREST, UTAH

FIELD NOTE

ROBERT G. ELLIOTT and **TURK OLIVER** manned the Pot Mountain Lookout on the Nez Perce–Clearwater National Forest, 1924. After spending many hours in the field dealing with fires, they met up with each other on the trail back to the lookout. Normally able to walk close to four miles an hour, they were going up the mountain at a slow pace due to hunger and being dead tired. About halfway up the mountain Turk saw an old rooster grouse walking across the trail. Turk made a beautiful head shot and Elliott offered to pick him and clean him. Turk said his frying pan still had bacon grease in it from a couple days earlier and he still had some bannock flour left. Elliott said, "Pretty soon we had fried grouse and bannock biscuits right in the trail and no meal ever tasted better. The old rooster was as tough as his years deserved, but man, was he good."

EARLY DAYS IN THE FOREST SERVICE, VOLUME 4, NORTHERN REGION

STORY & SONG

TRAIL CREW CAMP AT BASE OF DEAD HORSE PASS, WEST OF BLACKS FORK, WASATCH NATIONAL FOREST, UTAH.

TALKIN' SCALES

A cowboy and his banker met one day last week I'm told,
To talk about a loan until he got his calf-crop sold,
They got their business done alright, with very little fuss,
And then the banker had another item to discuss.

The banker said, "I note, my friend, you're skinny as a rail,
And you can see my portly form, I always seem to fail
To stick to any diet or to work out at the gym,
I'd like to know your secret, how you manage to say slim."

The cowboy said, "It ain't too hard to keep from gettin' plump,
A saddle, not a swivel chair is where I sit my rump,
And 'stead of punchin' keys on a computer every day,
I'm punchin' down and flankin' calves and buckin' bales of hay,
And rather than a three-martini lunch each afternoon,
I chew a hard-tack biscuit and I'm finished pretty soon."

The banker said, "I think I'd like to emulate your style,
I'll walk to work instead of drive, and it's about mile,
At noontime I'll go for a jog, though likely not too far,
And swap my three-martini lunch for one granola bar,
My secretary can assist, and I know just the way,
I'll chase her 'round the office carpet several times a day!"

"That's fine," the cowboy told him, "but there's one more thing,
    my friend,
Go get yourself a set of scales, hop on 'em now and then,
To check yer progress losin' weight if you want to begin
To slim yourself a little bit, reduce that big rear end,
And shed that hefty gut of yours, and lose a bunch of pounds,
It's worth it, man, although it may be tougher than it sounds."

The banker said, "It happens that I purchased yesterday
A brand-new set of talking scales to see how much I weigh,
My old scales had a dial down there, with numbers dim and small,
But with my belly hanging out I couldn't see at all,
So I bought their new modern ones that speak so I can hear
Exactly what I weigh, I guess, at least it's pretty near."

"Let's try 'em out," the cowboy said, "I never in my days
Heard of a scale that talks to me and tells me what I weigh."
He pulled his boots off, stepped aboard, and a pleasant voice
    did say,
"One hundred fifty-seven pounds is how much that you weigh."

"You hop on now," the cowboy said, "and let's see where you
    stand,
As you start your new diet and your exercizin' plan."
The banker did: the scale said, with a sputter and a cough,
"I think we've got a problem, all but one of you get off!"

STAN TIXIER, REGION 4, RETIRED REGIONAL FORESTER,
FROM A BETTER LOOKIN' HORSE

GRILLED PARMESAN POTATOES

Medium potatoes, unpeeled,
1 per person
Butter or margarine

Dash each of salt, pepper,
and garlic powder
Parmesan cheese

Wash and slice potatoes. Place potatoes on a piece of foil with 3 to 4 slices of butter, salt, pepper, garlic powder, and generous amount of Parmesan cheese. Fold foil at top and end to seal contents. Cook on grill or in campfire for 20–30 minutes, or until tender. They cook faster on the hot coals of a campfire.

LISA NEAMON-WILSON, REGION 8, LAND BETWEEN THE LAKES NATIONAL RECREATION AREA, KENTUCKY

FIELD NOTE

The Lochsa River Fire of 1929 was documented by ELERS KOCH in *Early Days in the Forest Service*, Volume I, Northern Region. Fire camp conditions were vividly described in the following paragraph:

"We were short on beds that night and the best I could find was a spare canvas fly to roll up in. I was at any rate glad to get back on the river where I could get a decent wash. I had been on the fire for fourteen days with no baggage save a towel and a pair of socks, and was indescribably filthy with the dust and sweat of the fire line. A fire camp is no place for a fastidious man. One learns to gladly tuck under one's chin the more or less dubious blankets a half dozen firefighters may have slept in, to drink out of a common cup or water bag with fifty men on the fire line, and to let the flunkeys slop great dipperfuls of food onto a tin plate with more than a little suspicion of grease on it and to devour it with appetite."

DUTCH OVEN SPUDS

¼ cup cooking oil
10 pounds Idaho potatoes
5 pounds white or yellow onions
¼ cup garlic powder
2 tablespoons chili powder

4 envelopes dry onion soup mix
Salt as needed
Pepper as desired
4 large bell peppers

Put oil in deep 14-inch Dutch oven and cover entire inside of pot. Scrub potatoes and cut off any bad spots; cut in half and slice without peeling. Remove outer layer from onions; cut in half and slice. Mix in garlic powder, chili powder, onion soup mix, salt, and pepper. Remove seed core from bell peppers; slice and dice. Mix well and cook over bed of hot charcoal, covering Dutch oven lid with charcoal as well. Stir about every 20 minutes, reaching to bottom of pot. Cook for 1½ hours or until done, whichever comes first. Serves about 30 people, depending on how hungry.

STAN TIXIER, REGION 4, RETIREE

CAMPERS ON YANKEE FORK NEAR SILVER CREEK, CHALLIS NATIONAL FOREST, IDAHO, 1939.

PARMESAN MASHED POTATOES

Make mashed potatoes the way you usually make them on a camping trip—either from scratch or using instant potatoes.

ADD:

½ cup sour cream
½ cup Parmesan cheese
½ teaspoon ground black pepper

Stir the sour cream, Parmesan cheese, and pepper into the potatoes until well blended and serve immediately.

JEAN MCNEILL, REGION 5, CALIFORNIA

CAMPING AT BIRD LAKE CAMPGROUND ON THE SOUTH SIDE OF MOUNT ADAMS, GIFFORD PINCHOT NATIONAL FOREST, WASHINGTON, AUGUST 1949. (PHOTO BY LELAND J. PRATER)

DUTCH OVEN BEANS

Soak 2 cups pinto beans for 24 hours; drain and rinse.

Into a 10-inch Dutch oven put the following:
2 cups soaked beans
2 onions, chopped
7 cloves garlic, crushed
2 tablespoons crushed red chile
1 small can diced green chiles or 3 fresh roasted and diced chiles
1 ham hock
½ teaspoon salt
1 teaspoon pepper

Cover with water. Put lid on tightly. Cook in 300-degree oven for 6–8 hours. Add more water as needed. When beans are soft, mash 3 to 4 times and add ⅛ cup brown sugar. Return to oven to continue cooking.

HUGH THOMPSON, REGION 4, RETIREE

FIELD NOTE

LYLE WATTS reported on the Forest Service Golden Anniversary dinner held at the Statler Hotel in Washington, D.C., on February 4, 1955. He described the candle-lighting ceremony, titled "The Blazed Trail," as follows:

"Bill Bergoffen narrated the progress for each of the five decades of past history of the Forest Service. At the proper point in the narration for each decade, one of the five candles on the standard was lighted. Mrs. Pinchot lighted the first candle, Ralph Hosmer the second, Earl Clapp the third, Lyle Watts the fourth, and Chief McArdle the fifth. A forestry school student dressed in field clothes lighted the candle to show the way for the next 50 years. It really was an impressive drama."

OLD TIMERS NEWS, *INTERMOUNTAIN REGION, JULY 1955*

BAKED BEANS

2 large cans of Bush's baked
  beans, vegetarian style
1 cup brown sugar
½ cup ketchup

¼ cup yellow prepared mustard
1 cup sliced green peppers
1 medium sliced onion

Pour all the ingredients into a 12-inch Dutch oven and stir together. Put
8 briquettes under and 15 briquettes over. Cook for 15 minutes. Remove
the bottom coals and simmer with the top coals only.

MARIAN JACKLIN, REGION 4, DIXIE NATIONAL FOREST, UTAH

TIP

When cooking vegetables, cover those that grow under
the ground and leave uncovered those that grow
above the ground.

GALE TAYLOR, ST. IGNACE, MICHIGAN, SEEING IF THE COFFEE HAS
STARTED TO BOIL. BREVORT LAKE CAMP AND PICNIC GROUND, REGION 9,
MARQUETTE NATIONAL FOREST, MORAN RANGER DISTRICT, MICHIGAN,
JULY 1939.

SIX BEAN CASSEROLE

½ pound bacon, diced
½ pound spicy Italian sausage, sliced
½ pound pepperoni, sliced
½ pound smoked kielbasa, sliced
1½ cups spicy barbecue sauce
1 can tomato soup
3 ounces tomato paste
½ cup brown sugar
1 (16-ounce) can pork and beans (undrained)
1 (16-ounce) can red kidney beans (undrained)
1 (16-ounce) can hot chili beans (undrained)
1 (16-ounce) can white kidney beans (drained)
1 (16-ounce) can lima beans (drained)
1 (16-ounce) can black beans (drained)

Fry bacon in Dutch oven until barely crisp. Add remaining ingredients. Simmer over coals until thoroughly warmed and flavors are well blended, approximately 30 minutes to 1 hour.

Susan McDaniel, Region 4, Regional Office, Utah

FIELD NOTE

CARL A. WEHOLT's memories from 1911 were recounted by Loyd Rupe and described harsh conditions in the Northern Region's Bitterroots. Both Weholt and Rupe were part of a crew assigned to open trails in the Elk Summit area and it "took rugged men to challenge the many traps that nature had set for those who pioneered its remote uncharted areas."

"The memory of wild game, fool hens, grouse, mosquitoes, blowflies, the sourdough jug that exploded in the middle of a pack, wonderful scenery, and comradeship, stuck with the men the rest of their lives."

Early Days in the Forest Service, Volume 4, Northern Region

BEAN HOLE BEANS

The art of cooking in a hole in the ground was used for hundreds of years by New England Native American tribes. This method was adopted by the northeastern logging industry as a way of cooking large quantities of beans for the woods' crews. Today, bean hole beans are still a popular northeastern tradition.

The ideal pot is a cast-iron kettle with lid or a Dutch oven. I use a #14 Dutch oven.

1. Dig a hole in the ground large enough to hold the pot with 2 or 3 inches of clearance on all sides, and at least 6 inches of clearance on top.

2. Build a fire in the hole with dry firewood and let it burn down to embers and ash while preparing the beans.

3. Parboil 2 quarts of dry beans (yellow eye or great northern work well) for 1 hour or until skins wrinkle. Drain off the liquid.

4. Slice 1 or 2 large onions and place in pot.

5. Pour in the beans.

6. Add several large slabs of salt pork or ¼ to ½ pound of bacon.

7. Add ¾ cup of molasses.

8. Add ¼ to ½ cup of brown sugar or maple syrup.

9. Add enough water to cover the beans—8 to 10 cups.

10. When fire has burned down, shovel out enough embers for the pot, and place the pot in the hole.

11. Ensure the lid is secure—if lid fits loosely, place a wet dish towel on top of uncovered pot and push lid down securely over towel.

12. Place embers around sides and on top of the pot. You may also cover these with dirt you removed from the hole you dug.

13. Cook for approximately 6 hours for delicious beans. Check beans periodically to ensure they haven't boiled dry, and add water as necessary.

If you dig the hole in an appropriate place, you can continue to use it for outdoor cooking. A truck rim works well for an expedient hole.

GARY C. MINER, REGION 9, WHITE MOUNTAIN NATIONAL FOREST, AMMONOOSUC-PEMIGEWASSET RANGER DISTRICT, NEW HAMPSHIRE

LONGHORN BEANS

1 pound bacon
2 (16-ounce) cans pork and beans
½ cup yellow onions, cut in pieces

SAUCE:
1 tablespoon vinegar

½ teaspoon prepared mustard
1 teaspoon black molasses
2½ tablespoons hickory
    barbecue sauce
½ cup brown sugar
¼ teaspoon crushed red pepper

Cook bacon until crisp. Pour off excess fat. Break bacon into small pieces and return to Dutch oven. Add pork and beans and onions to bacon. Mix sauce ingredients thoroughly in a bowl. Add sauce mix to Dutch oven and stir well. Cook for 35 minutes (10 briquettes on bottom, 12 on top). Stir once at 15 minutes. Rotate on coals at least once. Serve when beans are boiling well. Do not fill oven too near the top, as it will boil over easily.

LEE WHITMILL, GEOSPATIAL SERVICES TECHNOLOGY CENTER, UTAH

WASATCH NATIONAL FOREST, UTAH, 1930.

BASQUE GREEN BEANS

2 tablespoons olive oil
1 medium onion, chopped fine
1 clove garlic, sliced fine
2 (14½-ounce) cans green
  beans, drained, or 4½ cups
  fresh green beans
3 medium tomatoes, peeled and
  chopped or 1 (14½-ounce) can
  tomatoes, peeled and diced

¼ cup snipped fresh parsley or
  ½ teaspoon dried parsley leaves
1 teaspoon sugar
1 teaspoon salt
½ teaspoon dried basil leaves
⅛ teaspoon pepper
⅛ cup grated Parmesan cheese

Put olive oil in 12-inch Dutch oven and place on 10 to 12 charcoal
briquettes. Cook and stir onion and garlic in oil; add remaining
ingredients except cheese. Remove some of the charcoal and simmer
over low heat 15–20 minutes. Must bring to a boil, but do not overcook.
Remove from heat, sprinkle with small amount of Parmesan cheese, and
let sit with lid on for 5 minutes before serving. Do not stir after sprinkling
cheese on top. Serves 6 to 8 people.

THOMAS M. COLLINS, REGION 4, RETIREE

CAMPSITE LIMA BEANS

½ onion, chopped
1 tablespoon butter or margarine
2 (1-pound) cans lima
  beans, drained

1 small jar diced red pimentos
1 cup sour cream

Sauté onion in butter. When transparent, add lima beans and heat.
When beans are hot, add pimentos and sour cream and cook until heated
through. Don't boil, as the sour cream will curdle.

Excellent served with ham the first night out.

JEAN MCNEILL, REGION 5, CALIFORNIA

TIP

**Butter will keep indefinitely by submerging in a strong
salt solution, preferably in a sealed fruit jar. Keep in a
cool place.**

*CAMPERS AT BOILING SPRING CAMPGROUND, CLEVELAND NATIONAL
FOREST, CALIFORNIA. (PHOTO BY HUTCHINSON)*

ONIONS AND MUSHROOMS

2 large onions, sliced and
   separated into rings
1 pound portobello
   mushrooms, sliced

¼ cup (½ stick) butter or margarine
1 teaspoon garlic powder
¼ teaspoon salt
⅛ teaspoon pepper

Cut an 18-inch piece of heavy-duty aluminum foil into 4 squares. Place divided onion slices onto squares; place mushroom slices on top of onions. Dot each package with 1 tablespoon butter, and sprinkle with garlic powder, salt, and pepper. Fold aluminum foil, sealing edges. Cook on a grill over a bed of hot coals for 10–15 minutes on each side.

DIAN THOMAS, FROM RECIPES FOR ROUGHING IT EASY

FIELD NOTE

A timber sale on what is now Glacier National Park was the first winter assignment for R. L. WIESNER in 1909. He wrote,

"There was a ranger who was on furlough throughout the winter staying at the station here and I batched with him during my assignment on this sale. Generally speaking, we got along fine. There was some difference, however, in our ideas on the handling of the sourdough jar. He didn't believe it should ever be cleaned out. He said the 'green' that formed around the edges wouldn't hurt anyone. He also objected to dumping out the tea grounds because it took too much tea for the next brew if there were no old grounds to start with, and I was advised not to wash the frying pans as washing wore them out. He said he had used them for twenty years without washing them. I had no reason to doubt this statement."

EARLY DAYS IN THE FOREST SERVICE, VOLUME I, NORTHERN REGION

CHAMPAGNE STUFFED MUSHROOMS

20 medium fresh mushrooms
7 tablespoons softened butter
  or margarine, divided
4 green onions, chopped
3 tablespoons chopped
  walnuts, crushed
¼ teaspoon garlic salt

1 tablespoon parsley flakes
¼ teaspoon salt
⅛ teaspoon pepper
¾ cup Champagne or white
  (or blush) wine
Parmesan cheese

Wash mushrooms and remove stems. Chop the mushroom stems into small pieces. In a medium Dutch oven (10-inch) melt 2 tablespoons butter and sauté the stems. Halfway through cooking the stems, add the chopped onions. Once mushroom stems and onions are lightly cooked, remove from heat. In a small bowl, combine cooked stems and onions with the walnuts, garlic salt, parsley flakes, remaining 5 tablespoons butter, salt, and pepper. Mix thoroughly and then stuff each mushroom with the mixture. Arrange the stuffed mushrooms in the bottom of the Dutch oven, and add Champagne or wine to the bottom. Cover and bake for 30–40 minutes. Do not let the liquid boil away in the bottom of the Dutch oven. In the last 5 minutes of cooking, liberally sprinkle the tops of the mushrooms with Parmesan cheese and cover once again.

BILL LEVERE, REGION 4, REGIONAL OFFICE, UTAH, RETIREE

CAMPERS AT SOUTH BAY CAMP ON ELK LAKE, SOUTH SISTER IN BACKGROUND, DESCHUTES NATIONAL FOREST, OREGON, 1921.

NORTHERN
REGION FIRE
COOK CAMP.

FIELD NOTE

WILLIAM W. MORRIS remembered the Northern Region fires of 1910 and told of the following event, which occurred early in the season.

"We had been out of bread for some days and the packer had promised to relieve the situation on his next trip. Bread of some kind is essential to the happiness of camp life. We all were looking forward to the packer's coming. He finally arrived but reported that the pack horse carrying the bread had slipped off the trail on a steep rocky hillside, had rolled over a couple of times and the bread had scattered in all directions. The packer was able to get the horses on the trail again but had not stopped to retrieve the bread for fear he would lose track of the horses. Morris immediately set out to find the bread for the hungry workers.

"The loaves were scattered over more than an eighth of a mile and the hill was very steep. I had picked up possibly twenty loaves and was about to leave when I decided I would climb a tree and take a careful look around. Something caught my eye a way down the hill. I went down to it, and there was one of the boxes that had been packed on the pack horse. All around this box were scattered loaves of bread and I believe I must have picked up a dozen more at this place. This was quite a find, and I returned to camp with a bulging pack sack and rather proud of my ability to secure bread in the wilderness."

EARLY DAYS IN THE FOREST SERVICE, VOLUME I, NORTHERN REGION

BATTER FRIED EGGPLANT

1 cup flour
1 egg
1 teaspoon salt
½ cup milk or beer
1 medium eggplant, cut
   in ¼-inch slices
¼ cup oil

OPTIONAL:
½ teaspoon turmeric
½ teaspoon curry powder
½ teaspoon ginger

Mix flour, egg, spices, and milk or beer. Dip eggplant slices in mixture and fry in oil until brown on both sides. Drain on paper towels and salt to taste.

RICHA WILSON, REGION 4, REGIONAL OFFICE, UTAH

CAMPERS ON BELT CREEK, LEWIS AND CLARK NATIONAL FOREST, MONTANA, AUGUST 1922. (PHOTO BY K. D. SWAN)

GRILLED SQUASH

1 medium zucchini squash
2 small yellow squash
Salt and pepper

Garlic powder
Butter

Wash and prepare squash to cook on grill, cutting out any bad spots. Cut squash in long spears rather than slices. Place in the center of a piece of aluminum foil large enough to roll shut around the squash. Sprinkle with a small amount of salt, pepper, and garlic powder. Cut 2 to 3 slices from a stick of butter and place on top of squash. Roll aluminum foil shut in the center and then on the ends. Place on grill or on the hot coals in your campfire and cook for 10–15 minutes, or until tender. This will cook faster on the hot coals.

LISA NEAMON-WILSON, REGION 8, LAND BETWEEN THE LAKES NATIONAL RECREATION AREA, KENTUCKY

WILLIAM DESHLER AND HIS WIFE, ETHEL, ON BRIDGER PRIMITIVE TRAIL RIDE, BRIDGER NATIONAL FOREST, WYOMING, JULY 1959. (PHOTO BY CLINT DAVIS)

FIELD NOTE

ELSIE GODDEN, a country schoolteacher from Wisconsin, married her forest ranger (Floyd) in December 1928 and began a whole new life on the Lemhi National Forest in Idaho.

"Our home was a charming, old log ranger station with a wood stove and an old-fashioned heater in the living room. We carried our water from the creek.

"Floyd was a self-made man who could do almost anything. What he didn't know how to do, he tried anyway. I suspect that in the first year, he was trying me out to see if I was worth keeping. A ranger has many jobs. Since we were alone, I was called on to assist in all projects. When Floyd decided to raise a flag pole, I had to help balance it while he secured it safely. The garage was in the wrong place, so my job was to sit on the pry log while he got it ready to move. When the road needed dragging, I sat on the stone boat for extra weight. I weighed 105 pounds. Finally, I told Floyd he should have married a heavyweight, since he needed one so often.

"When spring came, we took to the hills, riding the range, counting cattle, checking salt licks, and seeing that the cattle were grazing in the right place. We had our pack horse to carry our tent, sleeping bag, supplies, and oats for the horses. Since a ranger feels that his horse is almost more valuable than his wife, we couldn't take many clean clothes. And in ten days, we got rather grubby. We packed our eggs in the oats to keep them from breaking. We lived on bacon, ham, eggs, fried potatoes, and a few cans of food. We rode all day and made camp each night before dark. We watched for fires, visited sheepherders, ate with road crews, and sometimes were lucky enough to stop at a ranch at dinner time. How I enjoyed those meals and visiting with the women.

"The ranger was a respected man in the community. The ranchers came to him with many problems. They didn't always trust each other, so when they sold a stack of hay they asked him to measure it. They also had him measure wood. I still have the formulas for hay and wood measurements in my cookbook."

OLD TIMERS NEWS, *INTERMOUNTAIN REGION*, OCTOBER 1970

BAKED CORN, DUTCH OVEN STYLE

7 to 8 slices bacon,
  sliced in quarters
1 large onion, chopped
1 medium to large green
  pepper, chopped
1 medium to large red
  pepper, chopped
4 eggs
2 (15-ounce) cans creamed corn

1 cup dry bread crumbs
2 teaspoons sugar
1 teaspoon salt
⅛ teaspoon pepper
Paprika (optional)
½ to ¾ cup cheddar cheese,
  grated (optional)
1 tablespoon parsley
  flakes (optional)

(Temperature: Equivalent of 350 degrees to 375 degrees)

In a medium (10-inch) Dutch oven, fry bacon until crisp. Remove bacon, let dry on paper towels, and crumble into small bits. Add chopped onion and peppers to hot bacon grease in the Dutch oven and cook until tender. While onion and peppers are cooking, beat eggs in a large bowl and add canned corn, bread crumbs, sugar, salt, pepper, and bacon bits. Once onion and peppers are tender, pour the corn mixture into the Dutch oven and stir. Sprinkle top with paprika and bake for 45 minutes, or bake for 45 minutes and sprinkle with grated cheese and parsley flakes the last 5 minutes of cooking. Be careful not to overcook on the bottom.

BILL LeVERE, REGION 4, REGIONAL OFFICE, UTAH, RETIREE

STOVE AT OUTDOOR
ASSOCIATION CAMP,
BIG COTTONWOOD
CANYON, WASATCH
NATIONAL FOREST,
UTAH, CIRCA 1940.

SIDE DISHES

BROWN RICE PILAF

2 tablespoons butter or margarine
1 small onion, minced
1 carrot, minced
8 cloves garlic, peeled and crushed

2 cups brown rice
1 lemon
6 cups chicken or vegetable broth

Heat a 12-inch Dutch oven over 9 hot coals. Melt butter or margarine and add onion, carrot, and garlic; cook for 5 minutes. Stir in rice and cook 5 more minutes. Add juice of 1 lemon and broth. Cover the Dutch oven lid and place 15 hot coals on top. Cook, covered, 50–60 minutes, or until all liquid is absorbed. Serves 6 to 8.

DIAN THOMAS, FROM RECIPES FOR ROUGHING IT EASY

FIELD NOTE

LUCILLE WEST JOHNSON recorded many interesting experiences while she and her Ranger husband, Irwin H. (Hap) Johnson, were stationed at the Pine Valley Ranger District on the Dixie National Forest in Utah. She wrote, "It was sort of an unwritten law in those days that the Ranger's wife would cook for the visiting Forest Service officials." She told of arranging for sack lunches for their noon meal while her husband hurriedly arranged for horses and other necessary equipment when several "official looking men" arrived for an unannounced inspection trip. "Since we could keep no fresh foods requiring refrigeration on hand, we used lots of canned meats. This particular day I used Spam to put in the sandwiches, and afterwards was told by the Ranger that just about all Forest Service men hated the very sight of Spam because it had been used so much in meals in CCC camps and by the US Army."

MEMORIES OF A FOREST RANGER'S WIFE, 1940-1946

SPANISH RICE

3 tablespoons olive oil
1 green pepper, diced
6 cloves garlic, minced
1 (15-ounce) can crushed tomatoes
2 cups rice, uncooked

1 teaspoon salt
2 ½ cups water
⅛ teaspoon saffron
   powder (optional)

Heat a 12-inch Dutch oven over 12 to 15 hot coals. Heat oil and add green pepper and garlic; cook until soft and add tomatoes. Cook, stirring occasionally, for 5 minutes. Add rice, salt, water, and saffron, blending well. Cook, covered, 15–25 minutes, or until rice has absorbed liquid. Serves 4 to 6.

DIAN THOMAS, FROM RECIPES FOR ROUGHING IT EASY

CAMPERS AT MIRROR LAKE, WASATCH NATIONAL FOREST, UTAH, AUGUST 1935. (PHOTO BY K. D. SWAN)

In August of 1952, the Old Timers of Ogden had a picnic at the Magpie picnic area about 20 miles up Ogden River. After returning from the picnic, GEORGE A. FISHER wrote about the picnic for the local newspapers. Fisher was a Uinta National Forest Ranger for 10 years. He ended his article with the following poem:

STORY & SONG

I want to go back to that Ranger shack,
To that cabin in the pines;
I want to hear as night draws near
The forest music chimes.

I want to feel that years can't steal
The peace in the pines I knew;
I want to hear with the old time cheer,
"Get off, we're about to chew."

I want to talk and I want to chalk
The dreams we had as we rode
Of paving the way for a better day
To a crowd coming down the road.

Let me go back to that Ranger shack,
To that cabin in the pines;
Please let me talk—maybe help me walk
Tow'rd that campfire and old times.

TIP

Make a master checklist. Before every outing, check the list to make sure you have every item. This includes planning menus and pre-preparing foods, wrapping them individually and freezing and/or drying when possible.

DIAN THOMAS, FROM RECIPES FOR ROUGHING IT EASY

NOODLES

1 egg

½ eggshell water

½ teaspoon salt

Flour enough to stiffen

Roll thin, let dry, turning 3 or 4 times. Cut in strips.

Boil chicken until meat comes off bone. Onion in broth.

Bob Williams. Recipe as dictated by Mary Youngblood, wife of Ranger Frank Youngblood, Council Ranger District, Payette National Forest, Idaho, 1957.

Zigzag River, Umpqua National Forest, Oregon.

MAIN DISHES

SPAM (YES, I SAID SPAM) CASSEROLE

1 (15-ounce) can new sliced
    potatoes (drained)
1 medium to large onion, chopped
1 (16-ounce) bag frozen peas
1 (12-ounce) can Spam canned meat
¼ cup margarine

¼ cup flour
½ teaspoon salt
¼ teaspoon pepper
2 cups milk
½ to 1 pound cheddar
    cheese, grated

(Temperature: Equivalent of 325 degrees to 350 degrees)

In a medium (10-inch) Dutch oven, combine potatoes, onion, and frozen peas. Slice Spam into ¼-inch slices and cover the entire top of the mixture. In a small (8-inch) Dutch oven, make a white sauce as follows: Melt margarine. Blend in flour, salt, and pepper. Cook until smooth and bubbly (being careful not to burn it). Gradually add milk, while attempting to keep white sauce as thick as possible. Heat until mixture boils and thickens, stirring constantly. Pour the white sauce over the Spam in the medium Dutch oven. Cover and bake (top and bottom) for 45 minutes. Sprinkle grated cheese over the top during the last 5 minutes of cooking.

BILL LEVERE, REGION 4, REGIONAL OFFICE, UTAH, RETIREE

FIELD NOTE

HARTLEY A. CALKINS entered the Service in 1914 as a draftsman in the Northern Region. One of his first field assignments was running a traverse along the Gravelly Range. The job was a transit survey to establish a baseline for future range surveys. Stone monuments were established at half-mile intervals. Calkins had two young fellows as assistants and a camp tender and cook, the latter part of the title being decidedly misrepresentative. He wrote, "I had always suspected that the man who occupied this position had had large experience as a sheep herder and that his culinary ability was limited to sour-dough biscuits and mutton stew."

EARLY DAYS IN THE FOREST SERVICE, VOLUME I, NORTHERN REGION

HOBO DINNER

2 carrots, peeled and thinly sliced
2 medium potatoes, peeled
   and thinly sliced
2 onions, sliced

1 pound ground beef,
   shaped into 4 patties
1 teaspoon salt
½ teaspoon pepper

Cut an 18-inch piece of heavy-duty aluminum foil into 4 squares. Divide vegetables into 4 equal portions. Layer with one-half carrots, potatoes, onions, and ground beef; finish with onions, potatoes, and carrots in that order. Season with salt and pepper. Fold aluminum foil and seal edges. Cook on a bed of hot coals for 15 minutes on each side.

Breast of chicken or fish fillets can be substituted for ground beef patties. Cooking time may need adjusting.

DIAN THOMAS, FROM RECIPES FOR ROUGHING IT EASY

TRUCKS USED BY CCC WORKERS AT BERRY CREEK CAMP F-3, NEVADA NATIONAL FOREST.

FLAUTAS

Pull apart precooked roast, chicken, or turkey into small strips. Sauté onions, tomato, and jalapeños (all chopped). Add meat strips. When tomato has cooked until mushy, put a tablespoon of meat mixture into middle of white corn tortilla, roll, and deep fry until golden brown. Repeat until you have used all the mixture. Serve any kind of salsa and sour cream on top. Eat with fingers. Yummy!

A good salsa to go on flautas is cooked and blended tomatillo and jalapeños, mixed with chopped raw onion, cilantro, a mashed ripe avocado, and sour cream.

MYRL ANN GUTIERREZ, REGION 4, HUMBOLDT-
TOIYABE NATIONAL FOREST, NEVADA

CAP BUETTNER FRYING SOME OF THE TROUT HE CAUGHT IN THE WOLF RIVER. TAKEN AT HIS CAMP ON THE BANK OF THE WOLF RIVER 1/4 MILE SOUTH OF LANGLADE, WISCONSIN, JULY 1964.

CAMP MEAL PREPARATION FOR SEEDING CREW AFTER 1910 FIRES ON THE CABINET RANGER DISTRICT, KOOTENAI NATIONAL FOREST, MONTANA, REGION 1.

 FIELD NOTE

ROBERT L. HESS was a scaler in the Northern Region and was working on a fire on the Kootenai National Forest in 1910. He wrote:

"I had only one old pack horse to pack water, equipment, and food, which was very limited, for 22 men. This was the latter part of August so one evening on my way to headquarters I cut across country in a hurry to inspect other fires, which were many, especially along the Great Northern Railroad. I was going down a sort of open ridge when I heard something and looked down a small spur of the main ridge and there stood a deer. And as we had no fresh meat of any kind (which was not furnished on small fires at that time, and very little at any time), and as I had a .22-caliber pistol with me, I thought I would take a chance at it. So I took careful aim, and at the crack of the pistol it dropped like a log. The next day the boys cooked the whole deer, and the pot never got cold until the deer was all gone, except for the reprimand I received from Washington, D.C. And later on I took it up with some of the higher-ups and asked them what they would do under the same conditions, and they said, 'O.K., but don't get caught.'"

EARLY DAYS IN THE FOREST SERVICE, *VOLUME I, NORTHERN REGION*

DEPRESSION BOLOGNA GRAVY

2 pounds beef bologna,
   chunk (not sliced)
2 to 3 tablespoons vegetable oil
4 ¾ cups water, divided

2 beef bouillon cubes
3 tablespoons cornstarch
½ teaspoon pepper
½ teaspoon browning sauce

Cut bologna into ¼-inch cubes. Heat vegetable oil in a medium (10-inch) Dutch oven, and lightly brown bologna. Add 4 cups water and bouillon cubes, and bring to a boil. In a small mixing bowl, combine cornstarch, remaining ¾ cup water, pepper, and browning sauce. Gradually add this mixture to the Dutch oven and boil gently for several minutes, stirring constantly. Serve over mashed potatoes, cooked rice, or noodles.

Bill LeVere, Region 4, Regional Office, Utah, retiree

Cornelia Pinchot cooking over campfire, USDA Forest Service, Grey Towers National Historic Site.

CHILI AND CHEESE HOT POT

3 (15-ounce) cans chili with beans
1 (7-ounce) can whole green
   chiles, cut into strips
3 cups beef broth

1 cups cheddar or Monterey
   Jack cheese, shredded
1 small onion, chopped
½ cup sour cream

Heat a 12-inch Dutch oven over 12 to 15 hot coals. Heat chili, green chiles, and broth until hot, 20–30 minutes. Divide into 4 to 6 soup bowls and top each bowl with cheese, chopped onion, and sour cream.

DIAN THOMAS, FROM RECIPES FOR ROUGHING IT EASY

DUTCH OVEN QUICHE

1 cup flour
½ teaspoon salt
⅓ cup margarine
4 tablespoons water
½ to 1 pound ground sausage
1 medium onion, chopped
1 green pepper, chopped

½ pound cheddar cheese, grated
2 large eggs
1 teaspoon parsley flakes
1 tablespoon flour
½ teaspoon salt
¼ teaspoon pepper
1 cup evaporated milk

In a medium bowl, combine flour and salt. Mix or cut the margarine into the flour mix. Add water a tablespoon at a time, and mix. Once mixture holds together in a ball, flatten with a rolling pin on a lightly floured board. Mold into a round pie crust and flatten it into the bottom and sides of a medium (10-inch) Dutch oven. Partially bake crust for 10–15 minutes, checking to make sure sides do not fall down. While crust is baking, brown sausage in separate small (8-inch) to medium (10-inch) Dutch oven. Midway through browning, add onion and green peppers. Once browned, spoon into partially baked crust. Sprinkle grated cheese over the top. In a separate bowl, beat eggs and add remaining ingredients. Mix well, and pour over the cheese. Bake for 30–40 minutes, until middle is cooked through.

BILL LEVERE, REGION 4, REGIONAL OFFICE, UTAH, RETIREE

POLISH SAUSAGE BAKE

1 tablespoon oil
6 boiling onions, peeled
   and cut in half
2 pounds Polish sausage,
   cut into 2-inch chunks
2 stalks celery, cut into 2-inch pieces
4 potatoes, peeled and quartered

4 carrots, peeled and
   cut into chunks
½ head of cabbage, cut
   into 2 or 3 wedges
1 cup chicken or vegetable broth
½ teaspoon salt
¼ teaspoon pepper

Heat a 12-inch Dutch oven over 12 to 15 hot coals and heat oil. Add onions and sausage and cook for 10 minutes, stirring until sausage has browned. Add celery, potatoes, carrots, and cabbage, stirring well. Cook, covered, for 30–40 minutes, until vegetables are tender, adding a little broth as needed to keep food moist. Salt and pepper and serve.

DIAN THOMAS, FROM RECIPES FOR ROUGHING IT EASY

CABINET IN NARROW PEAKS LOOKOUT TOWER, REGION 2, COLORADO, SEPTEMBER 1944.

While the couple above may just be filling a pan with drinking water from this source on the Targhee National Forest, in early days, dishes were washed in streams and lakes before pollution became such an important concern. In the photo on the right, two young women are using the beautiful Storm Mountain Picnic Area of Big Cottonwood Canyon, Wasatch National Forest, Utah, to wash and rinse their cooking utensils.

DUTCH OVEN STEW

Meat of your choice
Potatoes (enough for people
    you are cooking for)
Celery (enough for people
    you are cooking for)

Carrots (enough for people
    you are cooking for)
Mrs. Dash seasoning (to taste)
1 bag frozen cauliflower/
    broccoli/peas

Preheat 12-inch Dutch oven to temperature where fat pops. Brown meat and set aside. Place potatoes, celery, and carrots in Dutch oven. Season to taste with Mrs. Dash. Cover with water. Place meat on top. Simmer slowly until carrots are past crunchy. Add frozen cauliflower/broccoli/peas on top and simmer until done.

BILLY KEITH, REGION 4, RETIREE

FOREST RANGER LEROY SPRAGUE TALKING WITH CAMPERS DURING INSPECTION TRIP TO WARM LAKE CAMPGROUND, BOISE NATIONAL FOREST, IDAHO, AUGUST 1955. (PHOTO BY BLUFORD W. MUIR)

SON OF A GUN STEW

2 pounds bacon, cut into small pieces
3 pounds beef, cubed into ½-inch squares
1 teaspoon salt
1 teaspoon coarse ground black pepper
3 large yellow onions, cut into ¼-inch pieces
2 (28-ounce) cans peeled tomatoes
1 ½ cups soy sauce
1 teaspoon Accent seasoning
½ tablespoon garlic powder
½ teaspoon Kitchen Bouquet Browning & Seasoning Sauce
3 tablespoons Worcestershire sauce
¾ tablespoon crushed red pepper
3 green bell peppers, cut into ½-inch pieces
10 carrots, cut into thin pieces
10 celery stocks, cut into ½-inch pieces
11 potatoes, peeled and cut into ½-inch pieces

Cook bacon, beef, salt, black pepper, and onions until done. Mix tomatoes, soy sauce, Accent, garlic powder, Kitchen Bouquet, Worcestershire sauce, and crushed red pepper in a bowl. Add bowl mixture, green peppers, carrots, celery, and potatoes to meat and onions in Dutch oven and stir. Cook for 50 minutes (12 briquettes on the bottom, 14 on top). Stir about every 15 minutes. Rotate on coals at least once. Serve when potatoes are easily broken. Serves 8 ounces to 20 to 24 people.

Lee Whitmill, Geospatial Services Training Center, Utah

FIELD NOTE

"To be eligible as a ranger of any grade the applicant must be, first of all, thoroughly sound and able-bodied, capable of enduring hardships and of performing severe labor under trying conditions. Invalids seeking light out-of-door employment need not apply. No one may expect to pass the examination who is not already able to take care of himself and his horses in regions remote from settlement and supplies. He must be able to build trails and cabins and to pack in provisions without assistance."

Pinchot's book published in 1905, The Use of the National Forest Reserves

FIELD NOTE

From *Old Timers News*, Intermountain Region, June 1973, ARCHIE MURCHIE told of his sourdough experiences while snowshoeing on Idaho's Challis National Forest in 1941.

With his family settled at the Loon Creek Station, he would snowshoe over the summit once a month to bring in the mail and other provisions. A dog had adopted the family over the course of the year and, on this particular trip, had followed Murchie on his trip. He wrote:

"I had my sourdough in a quart jar, and for one person it was just the right size to mix up a good batch of sourdough hot cakes for breakfast. Before I went to bed I mixed up the sourdough. Then I remembered Old Bob (the dog) and figured he would be as hungry for some sourdough come midnight as I would be, so I added a little more of the makings. To keep the sourdough from freezing and have it warm enough to work good, I shoved it down along side of me between the two bags.

"A little before midnight I awoke and decided it was time to rise and shine. I raised up in bed and ran my arm down between the two sleeping bags to get the sourdough. I apparently had made one of three mistakes; I had either filled the jar too full, or it had been too warm and the sourdough had worked overtime, or I had not put the lid on tight! Maybe I had made a fourth mistake—I had gone to bed in my birthday clothes. Anyway, I ran my arm down between the two sleeping bags and I don't believe there is anything in the world to compare with the slippery, slimy feeling of warm sourdough. I pulled my arm out and it was dripping sourdough from my elbow to my fingertips.

"They say a good Ranger should be able to make quick, accurate, and sound decisions, but there I was trying to decide whether to try to get dressed in total darkness using one hand, ignore the sourdough and go ahead and get dressed, getting sourdough all over my clothes, or get out of bed and crawl to the door of the teepee, in my birthday clothes, with 0 degree weather outside and try to wash the sourdough off with snow. The latter decision prevailed. There was one frozen Ranger that finally crawled back into bed and shivered for a half hour before he got up enough courage to get up again."

VENISON STEW

½ cup flour
1 teaspoon each of the following:
   onion powder, garlic powder,
   seasoning salt, sage
2 pounds venison or elk,
   cut into cubes
2 tablespoons vegetable oil

1 pound carrots, cut into
   ½-inch chunks
5 large Idaho russet potatoes,
   cut into cubes
1 medium onion, cut into chunks
Salt and pepper to taste

Put the flour and the seasonings in a bowl and mix together. Dredge the meat in the mixture. Brown the meat in vegetable oil in a 12-inch Dutch oven and then add the veggies. Cover the mixture with water to the top of the ingredients. Cook with 8 briquettes on bottom and 15 briquettes on top until the spuds and carrots are tender to a fork, about 45 minutes. To thicken the broth, add some of the flour mixture to your liking. Salt and pepper to taste.

MARIAN JACKLIN, REGION 4, DIXIE NATIONAL FOREST, UTAH

FORESTERS CAMP AT MOUTH OF MONUMENT CREEK ON BELKNAP MEADOWS, WHERE CREEK JOINS POLE CREEK, BRIDGER NATIONAL FOREST, WYOMING, 1914. LEFT TO RIGHT: W. J. HAULEY, SUPERVISOR HALL, ASSISTANT DISTRICT FORESTER J. W. NELSON, RANGER BELKNAP, RANGER CANTLIN. (PHOTO BY W. C. BARNES)

PIONEER NIGHT STEW

1 large onion
1 potato per person
  (I usually use 10 to 12)
5 carrots, cut
2 (15-ounce) cans corn
3 pounds cubed game meat
  (I usually use moose)

3 to 5 tablespoons oil or lard
2 to 3 quarts water
3 bay leaves
Salt and pepper to taste
A little flour to thicken if needed

Clean all vegetables, cut into appropriate sizes, and set aside. Brown the meat in oil in a 14-inch Dutch oven, then add the vegetables, water, bay leaves, salt, and pepper. Depending on the weather conditions, this will take 1½–2 hours to cook. Remove bay leaves before serving.

Complete this dinner with loaves of sourdough bread.

KIM E. KIML, REGION 10, CHUGACH NATIONAL FOREST,
CORDOVA RANGER DISTRICT, ALASKA

PHOTO TAKEN AT SPRING 2004 SCIENCE CAMP OUTING IN ALASKA BY KIM KIML.

MILE HIGH STEW

(The best Dutch oven meal you ever had)

1½ pounds hamburger
2 quarts sliced potatoes, put in
   cold water until ready to use
1 quart diced carrots
1½ cups chopped onions

Salt and pepper
1½ pounds link sausage, cooked
   and cut into 4 pieces each
1½ pounds grated sharp cheese

Brown the hamburger in a 12- or 14-inch Dutch oven. Add the lightly
drained potatoes, carrots, onions, and salt and pepper. Mix and cover,
cooking until vegetables are done. Add the sausage and grated cheese,
(do not stir at this point); cover until the sausage is heated and the cheese
is melted. Use 15 charcoals under and 10 on top of oven.

DAN KRUTINA, REGION 4, RETIREE

FIELD NOTE

Legendary Forest Ranger RUDOLPH "ROSIE"
ROSENCRANS of the Blackrock Ranger Station, Teton
National Forest, was born in Austria in 1875. Rosie
came to the United States in 1894 and took out his first
citizenship papers in Hailey, Idaho. When he passed his
naturalization examination in 1904, Rosie was hired as
a forester at the Yellowstone Forest Preserve.

Many fine maps and plats drawn by Rosie reflect his
early European training and unusual handwriting skills.
His keen eyesight eventually failed after 23 years as
a Ranger and he retired in 1927. At the time of his
death in 1970, he was one of the few remaining charter
members of the Forest Service. His final resting place is
his beloved grounds at the Blackrock Ranger Station,
where a timbered ridge above the station will forever
bear his name, "Rosie's Ridge."

R4 INTERMOUNTAIN REPORTER, 10-2-70

MORONI GREEN CHILE STEW

3 to 4 pounds boneless pork, cut into 1-inch chunks
1 tablespoon olive oil
1 large (4- to 5-inch) sweet onion, chopped
6 large cloves garlic, crushed
2 (10-ounce) cans Mexican green tomatoes (tomatillos)
1 (8- to 12-ounce) can nopalitos (cactus pieces),
    rinsed well and coarsely chopped
¼ teaspoon ground cumin
1 to 2 cups chopped green chiles depending upon heat of chile and personal
    preference, or 3 (8-ounce) cans whole green chiles coarsely chopped
    plus 1 (8-ounce) can sliced jalapenos (optional substitute for jalapeños:
    2 tablespoons or about 3 medium diced canned hot chipotle peppers)
2 to 3 cups chicken broth
1 teaspoon oregano
3 chicken bouillon cubes or salt to taste
Freshly ground black pepper to taste
6 medium potatoes, pared, cubed, and boiled until not quite done
½ cup flour mixed in 1 cup cold water

Brown meat in skillet with olive oil. When meat is nearly browned,
add onions and sauté until softened. Put all ingredients except cooked
potatoes and flour in a 5-quart Crock-Pot. Cook on high 6–8 hours or low
8–12 hours. Add cooked potatoes the last hour (or use uncooked potatoes
and add with remainder of ingredients). Just before serving, stir in the
flour and water mixture. Allow to heat thoroughly and thicken. Serve
with warmed tortillas.

KEN STRAUSS, REGION 4, RETIREE

TIP

If soup is too salty, add slices of raw potato, boil, and
remove.

BOY SCOUT STEW

1 pound hamburger
1 (14-ounce) can each of green beans, mixed vegetables,
 corn, and diced tomatoes with the juices
2 (8-ounce) cans tomato sauce
Salt and pepper to taste

Brown the hamburger in a pot over the fire. Add green beans, mixed vegetables, corn, tomatoes, and tomato sauce. Add salt and pepper. Cook until heated through. Serves about 6.

My husband cooks this whenever we go camping and it is so easy.

LOLA LONG, REGION 4, ASHLEY NATIONAL FOREST,
FLAMING GORGE RANGER DISTRICT AND NATIONAL RECREATION AREA, UTAH

CAMP SCENE IN A NORWAY PINE GROVE. CAMPERS ON A CANOE TRIP. NOTE FIREPLACE CROSS STICKS, ETC., MADE OF GREEN WOOD. AS EVERYTHING MUST BE PACKED BY MAN, ALL FOODS USED ARE DRY. NOTICE OVAL-SHAPED BOX, WHICH IS FOUND VERY SATISFACTORY FOR TRANSPORTATION IN PACK SACK. REGION 9, SUPERIOR NATIONAL FOREST, MINNESOTA, JANUARY 1916.

BEEF STEW

2 pounds cubed roast
  beef or deer meat
1 cup flour
Salt and pepper
4 potatoes, cubed
4 carrots, sliced
1 stalk celery, sliced

1 bay leaf
1 beef cube
1 can beef broth
1 clove garlic, minced
2 (15-ounce) cans mixed vegetables
2 onions, chopped

Mix meat and flour, salt, and pepper. Stir until meat is covered with flour. Add all other ingredients in Dutch oven or crock pot. Slow cook. Do not stir until done.

Judy Boren, Region 8, Land Between the Lakes National Recreation Area, Kentucky

Lunch at Meadow Creek. Rangers Mendenhall, Thol, and Hutchinson, Flathead National Forest, Montana, February 27, 1927. (Photo by E. Thol)

PAUL'S CHILI

2 pounds pinto beans
4 pounds venison steak or stew meat
Bacon grease
1 small can diced green chiles
2 cloves garlic, minced
3 small cans whole or
   stewed tomatoes
3 medium onions, diced
3 teaspoons oregano, dried
2 tablespoons brown sugar

2 teaspoons cumin
2 whole red chiles, diced
1 teaspoon salt
3 bay leaves
1 teaspoon pepper
3 tablespoons chili powder
½ teaspoon sage
¼ teaspoon cayenne (optional)
Hot salsa to taste

The night before, soak beans. Drain, cover with water, and cook until tender. Brown venison or stew meat in bacon grease. Add to cooked beans. Add the rest of the ingredients to beans. Heat thoroughly. Better if made ahead of time and the flavors allowed to blend.

PAUL SHIELDS, REGION 4, RETIREE

FIELD NOTE

FRANK W. SEAMON wrote, "During the time I was in the Forest Service (1905 to 1939), I used 27 good horses, wore out four personally owned cars, and used several Forest Service pickups.

"I usually had two horses: a saddle horse and a pack horse. The pack horse carried grub, bedding, cooking utensils, and a fire tool kit. Fastened to the horn on my saddle was a double carrying case containing pencils, diary, maps, records, use book, and an automatic pistol. Many a native trout I caught early in the morn, cooked in the bake oven, and ate for breakfast. I washed the clothes I had on in the clear streams of water, dried them in the wind, and put them back on again."

OLD TIMERS NEWS, *INTERMOUNTAIN REGION, NOVEMBER 1958*

CHILE VERDE ENCHILADAS

2 pounds pork, diced
1 (15-ounce) can black beans
Cheese
Tortillas

1 large can green enchilada sauce
1 can green chiles (if you want
  this hot, use jalapeños)

Brown pork in Dutch oven. Roll up beans, pork, and cheese inside tortillas. Place in bottom of pan. Pour enchilada sauce on top of enchiladas, add more cheese to top of enchiladas. Cook for 1 hour.

BILLY KEITH, REGION 4, RETIREE

TENT CAMPERS AT CARDENS BLUFF CAMPGROUND ON THE SHORES OF WATAUGA LAKE, MR. AND MRS. ROY K. ESTEP, SONS WAYNE AND GLYN, OF ELIZABETHTON, TENNESSEE, CHEROKEE NATIONAL FOREST, TENNESSEE, MAY 1962. (PHOTO BY DAN TODD)

FAMILY PICNICKING AT SMOKEHOLE RECREATION AREA, REGION 9, MONONGAHELA NATIONAL FOREST, WEST VIRGINIA, JULY 1966.

CHILE VERDE

2 pounds pork, diced
1 can green chiles (if you want
  this hot, use jalapeños)

1 large can green enchilada sauce
Cheese
Tortillas

Brown pork in Dutch oven. Add green chiles and enchilada sauce. Cook for 1 hour at 350 degrees. Add cheese. Serve with warm flour tortillas.

BILLY KEITH, REGION 4, RETIREE

FIELD NOTE

WALTER G. MANN had high praise for his mentor, Guy B. Mains. In the *Old Timers News* of June 1970, he wrote, "Guy B. Mains was the Payette National Forest when I was there! I worked under him. He was a smooth diplomat. In later years his influence stuck to me. When I would have a difficult problem, I would say to myself—'Now how would Guy B. handle this?' The old timers are going but there are more old timers coming up."

FIELD NOTE

From the newsletter of the Old Timers Club, Intermountain Region, September 1952, CHARLES A. BEAM wrote of hard times during the winters of 1910 and 1911 on the Targhee National Forest in Idaho.

Dan Pack was Forest Supervisor and Beam was placed in charge of a crew of men whose job it was to build a bridge across Fall River. Shelter consisted of only small tents with no stoves in them to keep warm. The thermometer dropped to 42 degrees below zero and "many of our boys had frosted hands and feet. During this work a heavy snowfall came and completely buried several of the smaller tents and caused them to collapse in the middle of the night. They had to get out of these and were forced to stand around in the dark and snow until morning. Before fires could be started and tents reset, many of the boys received quite serious frost bites on their hands, feet, and faces. However, we succeeded in completing the bridge without the loss of any men. Then in the spring, Supervisor Pack was transferred to a Utah forest and Chester B. Morse was made Forest Supervisor.

"The following summer in 1911 we had a very large forest fire on Horse Creek. We had some 300 men working on this fire. One day when the men were all out on the fire line, a strong wind came up, and blew the fire out of control. It swept down the canyon and enveloped all the tents and wagons. Before all this equipment could be removed to safety, the cook tent burned down destroying most of the food supplies."

TIP

Baking soda has many uses in camp. It is an excellent fire extinguisher for flare-ups of the camp stove and soothing for burns. It also doubles as toothpaste.

CORNED BEEF AND CABBAGE

3 ½ to 4 ½ pounds corned beef brisket

8 cups water

2 teaspoons peppercorns

5 to 7 medium red potatoes, peeled and halved

6 medium carrots, peeled and sliced

1 cup brown sugar

¼ cup vinegar

1 large head cabbage

1 tablespoon salt

Wash the corned beef and place in a large (12-inch) or extra-large (14-inch) Dutch oven. Cover with water (add more if needed to completely cover meat). Bring to boil for about 5 minutes. Skim froth off surface, add peppercorns (or seasoning packet that came with the meat), and simmer 1 hour per pound. About 45 minutes before completion, skim water, and add potatoes and carrots. At end of cooking time, remove meat and pour a mixture of brown sugar and vinegar over top of the meat (keep meat temporarily warm in an alternate oven). Core and quarter the cabbage, and add it to the water in the Dutch oven. Add salt, and cook until cabbage is tender (30–40 minutes). Make sure you pour some of the liquid in the serving dish with the vegetables.

BILL LEVERE, REGION 4, REGIONAL OFFICE, RETIREE

FOREST SERVICE OFFICERS IN CAMP ON THE DESCHUTES NATIONAL FOREST, OREGON, CIRCA 1930.

MOM'S CHILI—SOUPED UP

1½ to 2 pounds ground beef
1 large onion, chopped
1 tablespoon vegetable oil
1 (30-ounce) can dark red
   kidney beans, undrained
1 large (46-ounce) can or
   bottle tomato juice

2 tablespoons chili powder
1 beef bouillon cube
½ teaspoon salt
¼ teaspoon pepper
1 to 2 green peppers,
   chopped (optional)
1 quart stewed tomatoes (optional)

In a large (12-inch) Dutch oven, brown ground beef and onion in vegetable oil. Once thoroughly cooked, stir in remaining ingredients and simmer, covered, 1 to 1½ hours. The longer it cooks, the more flavorful it becomes.

BILL LEVERE, REGION 4, REGIONAL OFFICE, UTAH, RETIREE

FIELD NOTE

In July 1909, JOHN S. BAIRD went to work for the Deerlodge National Forest in Montana and later transferred to the Superior and Minnesota National Forests in Minnesota in Region 9. In 1944 John wrote the following: "The differences between conditions in the Forest Service of 1905–1910 and those of the present day [1944] are too numerous to mention. There were no roads to speak of, not every ranger district had a station, and what stations there were, were log cabins. The astonishing thing is the fact that in spite of all this the Service got such a high type of men. The Rangers' wives may be given a lot of credit for this. They kept the stations spotless, and took good care of their men. I met a lot of rangers and their wives in my work, and I know. My hat is off to the old ranger and his wife. I truly believe that they laid the foundation of the Service."

EARLY DAYS IN THE FOREST SERVICE,
VOLUME I, NORTHERN REGION

BARBECUE BEEF AND BISCUIT BAKE

3 pounds coarsely ground
   beef (chili meat)
1 cup barbecue sauce
1 cup ketchup
½ teaspoon onion powder
½ teaspoon garlic powder

1 cup beef broth
2 cups sharp cheddar
   cheese, shredded
1 (7½-ounce) package buttermilk
   biscuits (10 biscuits)

Heat a 12-inch Dutch oven over 9 hot coals. Brown the ground beef. Pour off drippings and add barbecue sauce, ketchup, onion powder, garlic powder, and beef broth. Cook 10 minutes, until steaming. Sprinkle cheese on top and arrange biscuits on top of the cheese. Cover with lid and place 15 hot coals on top. Cook, covered, for 20 minutes, or until biscuits are golden brown and cooked through. Serves 8.

Dian Thomas, from Recipes for Roughing it Easy

Cleveland National Forest, California, 1922.

STERLING RIGHTEOUS JUSTICE, in his 1967 manuscript, recalls using pack boxes he devised and made himself, which he filled with provisions and utensils needed for meal preparation and carried on a horse or mule.

"The boxes had hinged lids and one had two horizontal shelves to hold cans, jars, or small dishes and utensils. The other box had no shelves and could be used for packing groceries. When ready to stop along the trail for a meal, all that was necessary was to remove the pack hitch, set the boxes on the ground, and start preparing the meal. The box having the shelves answered as a cupboard; the lid was the table, so everything, including a small telescoped cooking outfit, was ready for instant use."

Sterling, who started his career in central Idaho in 1908, slept in a small teepee when he went on pack trips. Teepees were light to carry and could withstand almost any kind of storm. A small Dutch oven was carried for baking and for other cooking. In his 1967 manuscript, Justice said, "Such items as flour, coffee, sugar, cured meats, dried beans, rice, and a limited amount of canned vegetables were carried. A few eggs were wrapped in paper, put into a tin box, and carried in a pack box."

Sterling Justice died October 30, 1980, in Nampa, Idaho, at the age of 96. He started work as a Forest Ranger on the Pocatello Ranger District of the Caribou National Forest, for salary of $2.50 per day. He was a District Ranger in the eastern Idaho area for 28 years. Justice Park, south of Pocatello, was named in his honor.

THE FOREST RANGER ON HORSEBACK, *STERLING R. JUSTICE*, 1967. USED BY PERMISSION OF *MARVIN JUSTICE, STERLING JUSTICE'S SON.*

TIP

Butter may be kept fresh by inserting it into the center of a sack of flour.

CHICKEN AND NOODLES

1 large egg
½ teaspoon salt
1 cup flour
⅛ cup milk
1 chicken, cut up

4 stalks celery, thinly sliced
1 large onion, chopped
1 dash of salt, or to taste
1 dash of pepper, or to taste

TO MAKE NOODLES: Mix egg, salt, flour, and milk until stiff dough forms. Cover and let rest for 10 minutes. Roll out until thin on floured surface. Let stand 20 minutes. Roll up dough jelly-roll fashion, leaving a heavy sprinkle of flour on the dough. Slice thinly and unroll the dough. Let sit about 2 hours.

While the noodles are drying, boil chicken in water—probably about 2 quarts. When chicken is cool enough to handle, remove skin and bones. Skim the fat from the broth. Return the chicken to the broth and add the celery, onion, and seasonings. Simmer for ½ hour or more. Add noodles and cook 20 minutes or until noodles are tender.

DALE AND CARMA BOSWORTH, WASHINGTON OFFICE, WASHINGTON, D.C.

NORTH FORK CAMPGROUND, SAWTOOTH NATIONAL FOREST, IDAHO, 1939.

PORK AND GREEN CHILE CASSEROLE

1½ pounds boneless pork, cut into ½-inch cubes
1 tablespoon cooking oil
1 (15-ounce) can black beans, drained and rinsed
1 (10¾-ounce) can condensed cream of chicken soup, undiluted

1 (14½-ounce) can diced tomatoes, undrained
1 (8-ounce) can diced green chiles
1 cup quick-cooking brown rice
¼ cup water
2 to 3 tablespoons salsa, or to taste
1 teaspoon ground cumin
½ cup shredded cheddar cheese

In Dutch oven, sauté pork in oil until no pink remains. Drain. Add the beans, soup, tomatoes, chiles, rice, water, salsa, and cumin. Cook and stir until bubbly. Place lid on Dutch oven and put coals on lid, and cook about an hour, or until pork is tender. Sprinkle with cheese and serve with flour tortillas.

GEORGE AND PAT ROETHER, REGION 4, RETIREES

TOURIST CAMP NEAR SOUTH ENTRANCE TO YELLOWSTONE NATIONAL PARK, WYOMING, 1924. (PHOTO BY BAKER)

SOUTHWEST CHILE ROAST

Roasting the ingredients on your outdoor grill gives this chile its full flavor and aroma for that great Western taste. Total cooking time is 3 hours. Serves 6.

½ pound pinto beans
6 cups water, divided
½ pound hamburger
½ pound bulk sausage
8 large New Mexico green chiles
1 large yellow sweet onion
8 cloves garlic
2 pounds Roma tomatoes

1 serrano chile
Olive oil
6 sprigs cilantro
1 lime, peeled
2 tablespoons brown sugar
Salt and freshly ground
    black pepper to taste

Bring beans and 3 cups water to boil in a large pot, reduce heat to simmer, and cover. Brown hamburger and sausage, drain, and add to beans.

Roast next five ingredients on an outdoor grill. Adding hickory or mesquite wood chips during roasting will enhance the smoky flavor. Frequently turn green chiles on grill until skin is blistered and partially blackened. To roast onion, peel, cut into ¾-inch-thick slices, brush with oil, and place directly on grill. Cook until onions are just soft and have black grill marks, turning once. Roast garlic until skin is light brown and contents soft. Frequently turn tomatoes on grill until skin begins to crack and change color. Roast serrano chile until skin just begins to turn color.

Remove blackened skin, stem, and seeds from green chiles. Tip: Place chiles in plastic bag for 10 minutes after roasting to help ease skin removal. Coarsely chop green chiles, onions, and tomatoes and add one half of this amount to the beans. Add the other half of the chiles, onions, and tomatoes to a blender or food processor along with the whole serrano chile (stem removed), cilantro sprigs, garlic, peeled lime, brown sugar, salt, and pepper. Blend until thoroughly mixed and add to the beans. Add the remaining 3 cups of water and continue to simmer, covered, for a total cooking time of 3 hours.

SCOTT EWERS, REGION 4, SPRING MOUNTAINS
NATIONAL RECREATION AREA, NEVADA

MAN'S BEST FRIEND HELPING HIM SET UP CAMP, SAWTOOTH NATIONAL FOREST, IDAHO, 1922.

STORY & SONG

THE VISIT

I ran into ole Zeke last week, we chewed the fat awhile,
I asked him 'bout his sister, and his face broke out a smile.
His sis lives in a town back east, a proper lady, she,
With plans to come and visit Zeke, and stay two weeks or three!

And Zeke had told me he weren't sure that he could tolerate
A visit lastin' all that long, but she had set a date
To fly from Boston to Cheyenne, and Zeke was quick to say
He thought he'd have about enough in no more than a day!

"And as it happened," Zeke allowed, "That's just how long she stayed,
She changed her plans and left next day, 'twas my fault, I'm afraid."
"Well, tell me then, how come the change?" I asked ole Zeke, and he
Explained it in a story he confided there to me:

"I met her at the airport in my old blue pickup truck,
Her luggage filled the bed clear up and it was only luck
That I had put the stock racks on and pulled out three spare
    tires,
Two saddles and my shoein' tools and several pairs of pliers.

"Back at the ranch that evening, well I cooked up quite a feast,
Dutch oven spuds and T-bone steaks, two inches thick at least.
There was fresh garden roastin' ears, some salad greens, then I
Outdid myself by bakin' up a deep-dish rhubarb pie!

"Well Sis, she bragged so on that meal, she said she'd never seen
A banquet quite so elegant, fit for a king or queen.
She said with all the work I'd done, the least that she could do
Was clear the table, fill the sink, and wash the dishes too.

"Oh no! sez I, you are my guest, besides I have a way
To clean the dishes, pots and pans, I use it every day."
With that I set the plates and bowls and platters on the floor,
With skillets, pans, and silverware and opened up the door.

"I whistled and I called the names of my blue heeler, Fury,
And my old coon-hound, Beauregard, and they came in a hurry.
Those two fine dogs did such a job, I wish you could'a seen,
In just about a minute flat, they licked the dishes clean,
And poor old Sis, although she tried to show her best restraint,
When those potlickers did their work, I feared that she might
    faint!

"Next mornin', Pard, she told me that she simply couldn't stay,
She had to visit Cousin Jane in Cody, right away,
And would I kindly drive her there? She asked me with a frown,
'Don't bother to fix breakfast, Dear, why we can eat in town!' "

STAN TIXIER, REGION 4, RETIRED REGIONAL FORESTER,
FROM A BETTER LOOKIN' HORSE

DUTCH OVEN ONE-POT MEAL

1½ to 2 pounds small to medium red potatoes, washed and unpeeled
2 medium heads cabbage, cut in wedges
3 onions, quartered
8 ears sweet corn on the cob, cleaned and broken in half
2 pounds smoked kielbasa or other smoked ring sausage, cut into quarters
1 quart water

Place the potatoes on the bottom of a 12-inch Dutch oven and layer as follows: cabbage wedges, onion, corn, and sausage. Add water and seat lid firmly on oven to keep in moisture. Cook for about 1 hour, with 10 to 12 charcoal briquettes on the bottom, replacing charcoal as needed. The smoky juice from the sausage drips down through the other food and gives it all a good flavor. Serve from the Dutch oven, or transfer some of the top layers of food to other containers for easier access to the potatoes on the bottom. Season to taste when eating. Serves 6 to 8 people.

THOMAS M. COLLINS, REGION 4, RETIREE

NOTE FROM TOM: I got this recipe from a horse packer in Montana. It is probably derived from the old cream can dinners that were used by early settlers in New England and the Midwest when feeding large numbers of workers at grain threshing bees, and other work parties. The food was layered in several 5-gallon cream cans. With the lids on, they were put on the coals of a wood fire to cook. When serving, the food was generally separated. The cook took the meat out (different kinds of smoked meat could be used), cut it up, and served it so everyone received some meat. This one-pot meal was a natural for Dutch ovens.

TIP

Remember, water boils at a lower temperature at higher altitudes and it is therefore necessary to boil longer than at lower altitudes.

FIESTA GRILLED HAM STEAKS

¾ cup jalapeño pepper jelly
2 cloves garlic, minced
¼ cup chopped cilantro

1 bone-in ham steak
(about 2 pounds)

Build fire and let burn until you have medium heat. In a small saucepan, heat jelly and garlic over medium heat until jelly is melted. Stir in cilantro. Set aside ¼ cup jelly mixture to serve at table.

Place ham steaks on grill over medium heat. Grill 3 minutes. Turn ham steaks and brush with half of remaining jelly mixture and continue to grill 3 minutes. Turn again and brush with remaining half of jelly mixture. Continue to grill 1–2 minutes or until ham is glazed and heated through. Serve with reserved jelly mixture. Serves 2 to 4.

JEAN MCNEILL, REGION 5, CALIFORNIA

COOKING MEAL
AT WILDERNESS
TRAIL RIDER
CAMP. FLATHEAD
NATIONAL FOREST,
BOB MARSHALL
WILDERNESS AREA,
MONTANA, JULY
1970. (PHOTO BY
B. R. VANGIESON)

CCC INSTALLING CAMPGROUND STOVE NEAR KETCHUM, IDAHO, SAWTOOTH NATIONAL FOREST, 1933. (PHOTO BY BRADY)

 FIELD NOTE

MARVIN JEPPESEN remembered good times working with Jim Jacobs on the old Lemhi National Forest in Idaho.

Once they were going to try some porcupine meat and about the time they were starting to prepare the meal, they were visited by two sheepherders and their dogs. One of the dogs managed to purloin their porcupine chops. Jeppesen said, "I think we were both very much relieved."

He wrote, "Late in the fall of 1932, we were putting up the wire on the new telephone line that was to connect the Pahsimeroi Ranger Station with the Mackay office. Our first camp was made in the foothills by a spring in the open sagebrush country." When time came to move camp, someone came and hauled their outfit up near the summit, but they didn't bring their stove. Because late fall brought the north wind, it became very chilly and although they had set up their tent, they still needed some heat. "We saw the remains of an old wrecked car in a gully, and managed to tear off part of it and flatten it out for a stove top. Rocks served as sides for the fire box. When we built the fire and started the meal cooking, the paint on the old car drove us choking out of the tent!"

OLD TIMERS NEWS, *INTERMOUNTAIN REGION, FEBRUARY 1968*

PACKER JOHN'S
SUPER BURGER

¼ pound hamburger
1 square aluminum foil
Salt and pepper
1 slice onion
⅓ cup fresh sliced mushrooms

1 hamburger bun (buttered)
1 slice cheese
1 slice tomato

Prepare hamburger patty, place on foil, and add salt and pepper to taste. Place onion and mushrooms on patty, fold foil, and seal ends. Cook on campfire (or in 375-degree oven) for approximately 20 minutes. Remove from foil, place on bun, add cheese and tomato.

PAM BARNETT, REGION 4, PAYETTE NATIONAL FOREST,
NEW MEADOWS RANGER DISTRICT, IDAHO

LOWER FIRE CAMP, BLACKWATER FIRE, SHOSHONE NATIONAL FOREST, WYOMING, AUGUST 1937. (PHOTO BY W. H. SHAFFER)

LASAGNA SURPRISE

1 pound ground venison (for the domesticated, hamburger can be substituted)
1 (32-ounce) jar homemade spaghetti sauce (substitute a jar of premade spaghetti sauce if you are in a hurry or just got lazy and didn't make any sauce)
¾ cup water
1 (6-ounce) can sliced mushrooms (drained, save water)
1 (6-ounce) can sliced olives (drained, save water)
1 box uncooked lasagna noodles
1 (12-ounce) container ricotta cheese
1 (12-ounce) container cottage cheese
1 (12-ounce) package grated mozzarella cheese
½ cup Parmesan cheese
Dried parsley

Brown meat. Mix with spaghetti sauce, water, and the water drained from the olives and mushrooms. Layer ingredients in a 12-inch Dutch oven in the following order:

1. About 1 cup of meat and spaghetti sauce mix
2. Uncooked lasagna
3. Ricotta cheese
4. Cottage cheese
5. Mozzarella cheese (save some for topping)
6. Parmesan cheese (save some for topping)
7. Mushrooms
8. Olives (save a few for later)
9. Sprinkle lightly with parsley

Repeat layering. Bake slowly at a modest 375 degrees for 1 hour. For heat place 9 briquettes on bottom and 12 briquettes on the top. Uncover and top with remaining mozzarella and Parmesan cheese. Sprinkle with parsley and a few sliced olives.

SHAWN W. ROBNETT, REGION 4, SAWTOOTH NATIONAL FOREST, IDAHO

NOTE FROM SHAWN: This is one of my favorite Dutch oven recipes I cook up every year at our family deer camp.

LEONARD'S FAMOUS STEAK FINGERS

Take one cup of flour, one egg, one cup of milk, and one teaspoon of baking powder, plus a pinch or two of salt (I reckon you could say salt to taste) and one full tablespoon of garlic. Combine in bowl and let sit while you take your favorite cut of hamburger (or steak if you are a GS-11 or above) and roll the hamburger out in small finger-like rolls. Then coat them in the batter.

Now, when I use a Dutch oven to heat the oil in, I use extra care if using charcoal or over a campfire so the oil doesn't get so hot that it catches on fire. When hot, slowly place the dipped meat in the hot oil. Cook them till they are golden brown to tan on both sides. Salt will tend to bring the garlic taste out so be careful of the amount of salt you use at this time. Place cooked meat on paper towels to soak up some of the grease. A raw potato cut into French fries can help keep the oil clean and makes for another side to your meal. I came up with this recipe sitting around thinking there had to be one more way to cook hamburger.

Leonard Roeber, Region 4, Boise National Forest, Idaho City Ranger District, Idaho

Mirror Lake, Wasatch National Forest, Utah, 1963.

TERIYAKI FLANK STEAK

½ cup sherry
½ cup soy sauce
¼ cup olive oil
¼ cup brown sugar
¼ cup fresh ginger, grated

2 or more cloves garlic, crushed
1 teaspoon ground black pepper
Chicken broth
1½ pounds beef flank steak

In a large, resealable plastic bag, mix the wine, soy sauce, olive oil, brown sugar, ginger, garlic, and pepper. Also add some chicken broth. Place steak in the bag, seal, and refrigerate 8 hours or overnight.

Remove steak from the bag and discard marinade. Cook on preheated grill on medium-high heat. After grilling, allow steak to sit about 5 minutes before slicing against the grain and serving.

KATHRYN HALAMANDARIS, REGION 4, MANTI-LA SAL NATIONAL FOREST, UTAH

FIELD NOTE

WALTER G. MANN told of his bucking horse in McCall, Idaho. The horse would stand still while the pack bags and top pack and bed were being put on but then the trouble began. A rope had to be put over the top and tied with a diamond hitch. Just as the rope was thrown over and before it could be tied, away he would go and buck everything off. This particular time in McCall, Mann had a supply of grub including a carton of matches. The horse ran and bucked all over town. He dumped the bedding, the sugar, and the flour, but the pack bags stayed with the saddle. Suddenly the matches in the bags caught fire and that was an exhibition—a bucking horse and smoke pouring out of the pack. Mann recalled, "Everyone yelled—that was fun for them, but not for me with my stuff scattered all over the country."

OLD TIMERS NEWS, INTERMOUNTAIN REGION, MARCH 1957

SWEET AND SOUR CHICKEN

1 (12-ounce) bottle of
  Russian dressing
1 (10-ounce) bottle of apricot jam

1 package dry onion soup mix
2 pounds boneless chicken tenders

Mix first three ingredients together and put tenders in to marinate for at least 1 hour. More is better. Pour all into a 12-inch Dutch oven and put 8 briquettes on the bottom and 15 briquettes on top. Cook for at least 40 minutes, then open the lid and stir to make sure all are cooking evenly. The chicken will be pink in color and it's hard to tell so check it out. If not, then keep cooking for at least 10–15 minutes. Yummy over rice.

MARIAN JACKLIN, REGION 4, DIXIE NATIONAL FOREST, UTAH

TRAILER AND CAMP SPOT, HOBACK CAMPGROUND, TETON NATIONAL FOREST, WYOMING, 1937.

DIAMOND–X DUTCH OVEN HOT WINGS

3 pounds segmented chicken wings
Peanut oil for deep frying
½ cup Louisiana Hot Sauce
½ cup teriyaki sauce
¼ cup brown sugar
2 tablespoons vegetable oil
⅛ teaspoon minced gingerroot

⅛ teaspoon cayenne
  pepper (or more)
⅛ teaspoon red pepper
  flakes (or more)
Lots of fresh garlic, chopped
  or minced (2 to 5 cloves
  or more, depending on
  how brave you are!!)

In a 10-quart Dutch oven, deep-fry wings in peanut oil until golden brown. Drain on paper towels. In a 2-quart Dutch oven, combine hot sauce, teriyaki sauce, brown sugar, vegetable oil, ginger, cayenne pepper, red pepper flakes, and garlic. Bring to a boil, then reduce heat and simmer uncovered for 10–15 minutes. In a separate Dutch oven, combine wings and sauce. Stir or toss until wings are evenly coated with sauce.

JARED S. MATTSON, REGION 4, CARIBOU-TARGHEE NATIONAL FOREST,
MONTPELIER/SODA SPRINGS RANGER DISTRICT, IDAHO

TOURISTS CAMPED AT BIG RIVER RANGER STATION, DESCHUTES NATIONAL FOREST, OREGON, AUGUST 1923. (PHOTO BY C. J. BUCK)

FIELD NOTE

DAN PACK, Palisades District Ranger's story

"THE SHOVEL METHOD"

In August of 1910, while fighting a fire in Darby Creek Canyon about 3 miles east of Driggs, Idaho, Ranger Dan Pack hired about 100 men and set up fire camp. He described the meal situation at camp as follows:

"The men were being paid by the hour and came in for meals at all hours of the day and night, with a relay of cooks to do the cooking. Our dishes consisted of tin plates, tin cups, cheap knives, forks, spoons, etc. The cooking equipment was very large galvanized tubs, wash boilers, five-gallon cans, and some large tin coffee pots. The campfire was never allowed to go out and as the men came in they gathered up their own dishes, went to the campfire, served themselves, ate their meal, threw their dishes into the dirty dish pile, and tried for a few hours of sleep."

Just as the Darby Creek Fire was being brought under control, another fire broke out on Badger Creek and it was necessary to move camp. However, the new camp with all of the cooking supplies was set up in the wrong location. When the food supply wagon from Driggs reached Pack, rather than send the driver further to the camp, Pack ordered him to unhitch. "It so happened that he had about a full carcass of beef and a few loaves of bread. When the men came in for supper we carved off some beefsteaks, used our long-handled shovels for a fry pan, and had bread and meat for supper. We didn't change the menu for breakfast."

Pack wrote that the Palisade was not free from fire for about 60 days and when the cooking equipment and dishes were returned to his office, "they were simply a lot of battered and burned utensils, hardly worth a dime."

INFORMATION CONTRIBUTED BY ANN KEYSOR, WILDLIFE BIOLOGIST ON THE CARIBOU-TARGHEE NATIONAL FOREST, MONTPELIER, IDAHO. DAN PACK WAS ANN'S GREAT-GRANDFATHER.

DAN'S SAUCY CHICKEN

6 to 8 boneless, skinless
   chicken breasts
2 tablespoons canola oil
1 medium onion, chopped
1 medium green pepper, chopped

⅓ cup cider vinegar
½ cup brown sugar
3 tablespoons soy sauce
1 (12-ounce) can tomato paste
½ cup mild salsa

Brown chicken in oil in a 12-inch Dutch oven. Combine rest of ingredients and pour over chicken. Simmer in Dutch oven until cooked (approximately 1 hour).

DAN KRUTINA, REGION 4, RETIREE

FIRE OBSERVER HELEN DOWE CLIMBING LADDER TO DEVIL'S HEAD LOOKOUT STATION, PIKE NATIONAL FOREST, COLORADO.

GRILLED HERB MARINATED CHICKEN

Breasts can be cooked whole, or cut to be assembled on kabobs. If putting on kabobs, slice chicken before marinating. This recipe is good with pasta, salad, and crusty bread.

¼ cup white wine (optional)
¼ cup olive oil
2 tablespoons lemon juice
2 tablespoons mustard
   (preferably specialty
   mustard, but any will do)
1 tablespoon Worcestershire sauce
2 drops Tabasco sauce

1 teaspoon onion powder
1 teaspoon garlic powder
2 teaspoons basil
1 teaspoon each of rosemary,
   thyme, and oregano
2 pounds chicken breasts
Enough water to cover chicken

In a resealable plastic bag, combine all ingredients except chicken and water. Mix well. Put chicken in the bag with the marinade. Add enough water so mixture covers chicken. Marinate overnight. If possible, turn bag over several times during marinating process. When ready to cook, remove chicken from marinade and grill whole or sliced and arranged on kabobs. Marinade can be used for basting while cooking. Chicken is done when juices run clear.

If no grill is available, wrap chicken in foil and throw onto hot coals.

Entire contents of marinade and chicken in a resealable plastic bag freezes well. This can extend the time chicken can remain in your cooler until cooking.

JENNIFER THEISEN, REGION 4, BOISE NATIONAL FOREST, IDAHO

TIP

Before heating milk in a saucepan, rinse pan in hot water and it will not scorch so easily.

ZESTY ITALIAN CHICKEN

4 to 6 skinless and boneless chicken breasts
1 (16-ounce) bottle zesty Italian salad dressing

Wash chicken breasts and prepare them to marinate the night before you wish to cook them. Place the chicken breasts flat in a sealable container while pouring ½ of the zesty Italian dressing over them; pierce the chicken breasts with a fork. Turn the chicken breasts over and repeat this on the other side. Place in the refrigerator and allow to sit overnight. Turn the chicken 3 or 4 times before cooking. Grill on each side for approximately 10 minutes until well cooked.

LISA NEAMON-WILSON, REGION 8, LAND BETWEEN THE LAKES NATIONAL RECREATION AREA, KENTUCKY

TIMBER CRUISING CREW, TETON NATIONAL FOREST, WYOMING, 1924. (PHOTO BY ERWIN G. WIESEHUEGEL)

THE CIVILIAN CONSERVATION CORPS (CCC) was established in 1933 as part of President Roosevelt's New Deal Initiative. Agencies that participated along with the Forest Service in this successful program were the Army, the Department of Labor, the Soil Conservation Service, and the Department of Interior. Many CCC enrollees came from eastern states and the program utilized agency employees to train, supervise, and mentor hundreds of unskilled young men. The enrollees provided manpower to construct roads, bridges, campgrounds, and many other important projects. Young men thinned trees, built signs and other structures, repaired and rebuilt telephone lines, and learned skills that enabled many of them to become professional foresters. One of the most important contributions was their manpower used to prevent and control forest fires.

CCC BOYS FROM CAMP F-25 LEAVING FOR INDIAN CREEK FIRE ON THE BRIDGER-TETON NATIONAL FOREST, WYOMING, 1937. (PHOTO BY W. H. SHAFFER)

PISTOL ROCK CHICKEN

1 whole chicken, skinned
  and cut into pieces
½ teaspoon salt
¼ teaspoon pepper
⅛ teaspoon garlic salt

1 cup all-purpose flour
2 tablespoons oil
1 (15-ounce) can crushed tomatoes
1 (8-ounce) can sliced
  mushrooms, drained

Rinse chicken thoroughly and pat dry with paper towels. In a 1-gallon plastic resealable bag, add salt, pepper, garlic salt, and flour. Add chicken, close the bag, and shake well to coat. Place a 12-inch Dutch oven over 12 to 15 hot coals. Add oil to hot Dutch oven and brown chicken well on all sides. Pour off excess oil and add tomatoes and mushrooms. Simmer, covered, stirring occasionally, for 1 hour. Remove cover and cook 15 minutes, until sauce thickens, stirring frequently. Serves 4.

DIAN THOMAS, FROM RECIPES FOR ROUGHING IT EASY

STOVE AND FOOD STORAGE SET UP AT SADDLE MOUNTAIN FIRE BASE CAMP, BITTERROOT NATIONAL FOREST, MONTANA, JULY 1960. (PHOTO BY W. E. STEUERWALD)

DUTCH OVEN CHICKEN MARSALA

6 boneless chicken breasts
Olive oil
1½ cups Marsala wine
1½ cups mushrooms, thinly sliced
1 cup sweet red pepper, julienned
1 cup sweet yellow pepper, julienned
½ cup green onions

2 cloves garlic
3 cups chicken broth, divided
½ teaspoon each of dried oregano and dried basil
1 teaspoon salt
Fresh ground black pepper
1 tablespoon lemon juice
1 tablespoon cornstarch

Cut chicken into strips. Add olive oil to Dutch oven and heat until hot. Place chicken in Dutch oven and sauté until tender. Remove and set aside. Add wine to Dutch oven and bring to a boil, then pour it over the chicken. Add more olive oil to oven, heat until hot, and then add mushrooms, peppers, green onions, and garlic and sauté until tender. Add 2¾ cups chicken broth with herbs and lemon juice. Combine cornstarch with the remaining ¼ cup chicken broth and add to Dutch oven, then boil about 1 minute until thickened. Return the chicken and wine to oven and cook until heated through.

Serve with pasta.

KATHRYN HALAMANDARIS, REGION 4, MANTI-LA SAL NATIONAL FOREST, UTAH

STORY & SONG

I like Forest Service coffee,
Think it's mighty fine.
Good for cuts and bruises,
Just like iodine.

I like Forest Service biscuits,
Think they're mighty fine.
One rolled off the table,
And killed a pal of mine.

I like Forest Service corned beef,
It really is okay.
I fed it to the ground squirrels,
Funerals are today!

PART OF THE "LOOKOUT BALLAD," WRITTEN BY A BORED FIRE LOOKOUT ON THE COLVILLE NATIONAL FOREST, WASHINGTON, 1948

CHICKEN AND SALSA OLÉ

½ cup all-purpose flour
½ teaspoon salt
½ teaspoon chili powder
½ teaspoon garlic powder
6 to 8 chicken breasts,
  boned and skinned

2 tablespoons oil
2 (7-ounce) cans chiles
2 cups cheddar cheese, shredded
1 (14- to 20-ounce) jar salsa

In a 1-gallon resealable plastic bag, mix flour, salt, chili powder, and garlic powder; shake the chicken in the bag. Heat a 12-inch Dutch oven over 12 to 15 hot coals. Heat oil and add chicken pieces. Cook on each side for 10 minutes. Split chiles open and place one on top of each chicken breast. Sprinkle each with ½ cup cheese. Pour salsa around the chicken and cook, covered, for 5 minutes, until heated thoroughly and cheese is melted. Serve with tortillas and refried beans or Spanish rice. Serves 6 to 8.

DIAN THOMAS, FROM RECIPES FOR ROUGHING IT EASY

THE MAZAMAS OUTING CLUB OF PORTLAND, OREGON, ENJOYING MEAL AT LITTLE REDFISH LAKE, SAWTOOTH NATIONAL FOREST, IDAHO, 1940.

DUTCH OVEN BAKED CHICKEN

1 whole chicken (cut in pieces)
5 large potatoes (cut in large chunks)
1 onion (quartered)
Salt and pepper to taste
1 cup water

Place the chicken in a Dutch oven. Add potatoes, onion, salt, pepper, and water. Cover and cook over open flame, not too close or it will burn. Cook slowly for about 1 hour. Keep a watch on the water—add a little as it cooks to keep from burning. Add pan biscuits baked on coals around flame and you have a complete meal.

TERRI VINING, REGION 8, OZARK-ST. FRANCIS NATIONAL FORESTS, ARKANSAS, RETIREE

CAMP STOVE, CIRCA 1935.

FIELD NOTE

ERWIN G. WIESEHUEGEL recollected early-day experiences of the Wyoming (later the Bridger-Teton National Forest in Wyoming) and the Uinta National Forest in Utah. He recalled "the ranger meeting at Afton when Leo Fest and I had to pull our mattress to the floor of the hotel room because we couldn't sleep on a soft bed after becoming so accustomed to the hard earth and the bare floor of his ranger station." He also mentioned the "disposition of stills Ed Adair and I found on the Uinta. Such was the life then."

OLD TIMERS NEWS, OCTOBER 1981

PONDEROSA PICNIC AREA ON BEAVER CREEK, FISHLAKE NATIONAL FOREST, UTAH, SEPTEMBER 1945. (PHOTO BY P. S. BIELER)

BEER ROASTED CHICKEN

1 medium onion, peeled
1 (3- to 5-pound) roasting chicken
Fresh herbs: parsley, sage, rosemary, and thyme (sounds like a song to me)
2 cans of good beer

Place peeled onion inside the chicken's cavity, then put fresh herbs in and around the chicken. Place chicken in 12-inch Dutch oven. Pour 1 can of beer over the chicken and put the lid on; place 8 briquettes underneath and 15 briquettes on top. Cook for 1 hour. Check at 30 minutes to make sure it's cooking. You may need to put fresh briquettes on after you open. The second can of beer can be drunk while you are waiting for the chicken to be done.

MARIAN JACKLIN, REGION 4, DIXIE NATIONAL FOREST, UTAH

DUTCH OVEN PARMESAN CHICKEN

3 pounds broiler-fryer chicken,
   skinned and cut up
1¼ cups grated Parmesan cheese

1 teaspoon salt
¼ teaspoon pepper
⅓ cup butter or margarine, melted

Remove skin and cut chicken into pieces. Mix cheese, salt, and pepper. Dip chicken into butter, then coat with cheese mixture. Place chicken in 12-inch Dutch oven. Cover with coals and cook 45–50 minutes or until golden brown. Makes 4 servings.

MICHELE HUFFMAN, REGION 4, ASHLEY NATIONAL FOREST, UTAH

TIP

Keep butter or margarine for a long time by packing it in sterilized jars with tight fitting, screw-top lids.

PICNICKING AT NORWAY BEACH ON CASS LAKE, CHIPPEWA NATIONAL FOREST, MINNESOTA, MAY 1917. (PHOTO BY W. J. HUTCHINSON)

Early in EARL V. WELTON's career on the old Helena National Forest he made a trip to the vicinity of the Emery Mine, located ten miles east of Deer Lodge. He stopped around the noon hours at the cabin of some miners but did not find them home. He spied an open box of apples, took a couple, and rode on. That afternoon he came past the place where the men were working and accepted their invitation to spend the night with them back at their cabin. In his memoir recorded in the Northern Region's *Early Days in the Forest Service*, Volume I, he wrote:

"Some time after supper one of the men went to the apple box to get some apples to pass around. There wasn't an apple in the box. They had all been taken from the box sometime that afternoon. A hunt for the apples began at once, for we thought they must be somewhere in the house. There were two rooms in the cabin. The front room, used as a kitchen, was fully completed. The back room, which served as a bedroom, was not ceiled [*sic*] overhead, which left a space between the bottom of each rafter on the plate. We finally found the apples, all lined up, one beside the other, along the plates between the rafters. They had been placed there, one by one, by a single pack rat, between 1:30 and 5:00. Needless to say, we dispatched the rat."

GRANITEWARE USED AT IRON MOUNTAIN LOOKOUT, SAWTOOTH NATIONAL FOREST, IDAHO, CIRCA 1930.

SWEET AND SOUR CHICKEN

Chicken, pork spareribs,
  or beef short ribs
3 large cans tomato sauce
1 quart water
1 large can chunk pineapple

Liquid smoke to taste
Worcestershire sauce to taste
Salt
1½ cups brown sugar
Flour or cornstarch for thickening

Place meat in 12- or 14-inch Dutch oven until ¾ full. Brown if using ribs.
Mix tomato sauce, water, pineapple, liquid smoke, Worcestershire sauce,
salt, and brown sugar and pour over meat. For uniform heat, place 12 to
14 charcoal briquettes below the Dutch oven and the same on top. Cook
meat till nearly done, about 45 minutes. To thicken the sauce after the
meat is nearly done, make a thickening agent of flour and water or
cornstarch and water. Add 3 to 4 cups to the Dutch oven and stir in with
the meat. Cook until sauce is thickened and meat is done. The sauce is
good on baked potatoes.

CRAIG AND MARY GREENE, REGION 4, RETIREES

*COOKSTOVE USED IN SETH BULLOCK LOOKOUT, REGION 2,
COLORADO, AUGUST 1944.*

POTATO CHICKEN CASSEROLE

½ pound bacon, cut into chunks
8 to 10 boneless, skinless
   chicken breast halves
2 medium onions, chopped
1 can mushrooms, drained
1½ teaspoons poultry
   seasoning, divided
12 to 14 medium potatoes,
   peeled and sliced

1 (10-ounce) can cream
   of chicken soup
1 (10-ounce) can cream
   of celery soup
1 cup sour cream
1½ teaspoons seasoning salt
½ teaspoon garlic salt
Salt and pepper to taste
2 cups grated cheddar cheese

Heat a 12-inch Dutch oven until hot. Fry bacon until brown. Cut chicken into bite-size pieces. Add chicken, onions, mushrooms, and ½ teaspoon of the poultry seasoning. Stir, then cover and cook until onions are translucent and chicken is tender. Add potatoes. Stir in soups, sour cream, and the remaining seasonings. Cover and cook for 45–60 minutes using 8 to 10 coals on the bottom and 14 to 16 coals on the top. Stir every 10–15 minutes. When done, cover top with cheese and replace lid. Let stand until cheese is melted.

Bob VanGieson, Region I, retiree

Wasatch National Forest, Utah, 1930. (Photo by Shipp)

OVEN SMOKED TURKEY

½ cup table salt
1 cup Morton Tender
  Quick seasoning
1 gallon cold water

1 (3½- to 4-ounce) bottle
  liquid smoke
12- to 14-pound turkey

Use a non-metal container large enough to brine the turkey—a small plastic pail works very well. Dissolve salt and seasoning in water; add liquid smoke. Place bird, head first, into the brine; be certain cavity fills. Add more water to cover if necessary. Soak bird in brine for 24 hours at room temperature. Drain bird, place breast-down in V-rack over a shallow pan. Roast for 12 hours at 250 degrees. Remove from oven and slide pan and all into 2 brown paper bags (1 from each direction) to hold smoky flavor in the meat as it cools. If you have a big bag and a small turkey you can use 1 bag; just fold and staple the opening. When cool enough to handle (30–45 minutes), skin, debone, slice, and serve. Freezes very well. The dark meat falls off the bones in chunks; the breast is best when cold.

PLANNING: This recipe is so simple, sometimes it's easy to forget how long it takes. Note on the calendar when you want to serve it, then count backwards. I allow 40 hours for a fresh bird. Be sure to include defrosting time.

DALENE LEMBERES, REGION 4, PAYETTE NATIONAL FOREST, IDAHO

FIELD
NOTE

When WILLIAM "BILL" F. TRIBE retired in October 1952, he left a career that took him to many locations throughout the country. In the summer of 1916, he brought his bride to a two-room cabin at Black's Fork on the Wasatch National Forest. Mary Tribe enjoyed roughing it in the summer but found Utah's winter temperature dropped to 32 degrees below zero. "It was cold inside the cabin as well as out, and water carried from a hole in the ice-covered creek would freeze if spilled on the floor. Frying an egg meant peeling the shell from a frozen egg, dropping it in the skillet and waiting for it to thaw out."

OLD TIMERS NEWS, INTERMOUNTAIN REGION, MARCH 1953

DUTCH OVEN ORANGE GLAZED STUFFED PORK CHOPS

1 cup celery, diced small
1½ cups onion, diced small
¾ cup butter
2 cups bread cubes, cut
    in 1-inch cubes
2 tablespoons parsley, chopped
¼ cup almonds, slivered
1 to 2 apples, peeled,
    cored, and diced
1 teaspoon allspice
1 teaspoon rosemary
1½ cups water
10 pork chops, 8 ounces each
    with pockets cut (I use Hormel
    injected pork, extra thick
    with the bone [tail] left on)

2 teaspoons salt
2 teaspoons pepper, fresh ground
1 teaspoon paprika
2 to 4 ounces olive oil

GLAZE:
Zest and juice from 4 oranges
2 cups sugar
2 teaspoons ground cinnamon
1 teaspoon salt
4 tablespoons cornstarch
15 to 20 whole cloves
Garnish: parsley, orange slices,
    maraschino cherries, kale or curly
    lettuce, bell pepper, green onions

Sauté the celery and onion in half of the butter until tender. Combine the celery, onions, and remaining butter with the bread cubes, parsley, almonds, apples, allspice, and rosemary. Add enough water to moisten the dressing. Stuff the mixture into the pork chops. Seal the pockets with toothpicks and tie with butcher string. Using a 14-inch Dutch oven, sprinkle chops with salt, pepper, and paprika and brown the chops in olive oil on each side. Add the water, bring to a simmer, and cook at about 350 degrees until tender (12 coals on the bottom and 16 to 18 on top). Meat should register 175 degrees. Meanwhile, prepare the glaze and simmer until thickened. Remove the chops from the pan, dip in the glaze and place on the lid lined with kale for presentation. To serve, garnish with parsley, green onions, orange slices, and cherries. Pour the remaining glaze over the chops and into a bell pepper that has the top cut off. Serves 10.

DAN KRUTINA, REGION 4, RETIREE

PORK ROAST WITH BLACK-EYED PEAS

½ pound bacon, quartered
1 large onion, chopped
4 to 6 pounds boneless pork roast
Meat tenderizer
Salt and pepper
2 cloves garlic, finely
  chopped or pressed

½ cup water
2 (15-ounce) cans black-
  eyed peas (undrained)
1 (15-ounce) can dark red
  kidney beans (undrained)
1½ to 2 tablespoons chili powder

(Temperature: equivalent of about 350 degrees to 375 degrees)

Lightly brown bacon in a large 12-inch Dutch oven (do not drain). Add onion and cook about 5 minutes longer. Prepare pork roast—sprinkle with tenderizer, salt, and pepper on both sides. Put two chopped or pressed garlic cloves on top of the roast—spread on top. Put bacon and onions to sides of Dutch oven and put the roast in the middle. Add up to ½ cup water to keep the roast moist. Cover and cook 1½–2 hours. Make sure that the bottom of the Dutch oven stays moist—add slightly more water as needed. When the roast is almost cooked, add the black-eyed peas and kidney beans. Add ½ teaspoon salt, ¼ teaspoon pepper, and chili powder to the peas and beans. Sprinkle some chili powder on top of roast. Cook about 1 hour longer. Transfer roast to cutting board and slice. Serve sliced pork in juices with the peas and beans on the side.

BILL LEVERE, REGION 4, REGIONAL OFFICE, UTAH, RETIREE

CRESCENT LAKE, DESCHUTES NATIONAL FOREST, OREGON, 1920.

CURT'S MOUTH-WATERIN' BARBECUE RIBS

Small amount vegetable oil
Boneless country-style pork or beef ribs (quantity depends on size of Dutch oven)
Salt and pepper and favorite seasonings
1 large green pepper, seeded and sliced
1 large red pepper, seeded and sliced
1 large yellow pepper, seeded and sliced
1 large orange pepper, seeded and sliced
1 large yellow onion, sliced
1 to 2 bottles of favorite barbecue sauce (recommend at least one good quality one)
1 (32-ounce) bottle lemon-lime soda

Preheat Dutch oven (can be on a Cache-cooker or open fire). Add vegetable oil—enough to coat bottom. Brown the ribs in Dutch oven (may only be able to brown a few at a time). Once ribs are browned, remove Dutch oven from heat and place all the ribs in oven. Sprinkle with salt and pepper and seasonings. Add peppers and onion (spread them out a bit). Cover ribs with the barbecue sauce. Add some of the lemon-lime soda to cover bottom layer of ribs at least. Place lid on Dutch oven and return to heat; allow ribs to simmer on medium heat. Check and stir occasionally to ensure that there is enough moisture so ribs are simmering in sauce. Ribs will be done when you can easily cut them with a fork or spatula (may take 1–2 hours). Serve with Dutch oven taters.

Note from Curt: This is a local favorite that I have made several times for various District occasions. I created this recipe while spiked out with a timber crew during my days as a seasonal in the mid-1990s. Then word spread and I ended up making them for two different districts and for two good friends when they had going-away parties.

CURTIS KEETCH, REGION 4, CARIBOU-TARGHEE NATIONAL FOREST, DUBOIS RANGER DISTRICT, IDAHO

TIP

Use resealable plastic bags for handy packing—then dispose of properly.

THIS PHOTOGRAPH TAKEN BY K. D. SWAN IN THE MID 1930s SHOWS HOW SUPPLIES WERE CAREFULLY PACKED BEFORE BEING DROPPED BY AIR INTO NORTHERN REGION FIRE CAMPS.

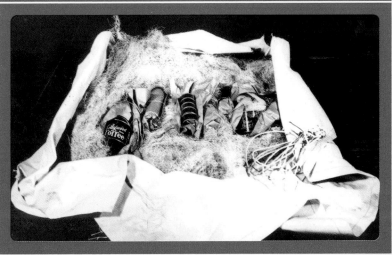

In 1940 in the Kootenai National Forest, ERNIE RICHARDS was asked to help drop cargo out of a trimotor Ford airplane for the Bull Lake Fire. After pilot Dick Johnson had circled the area a couple of times to become familiar with the drop spot, Ernie started dropping the cargo. Right after kicking out the first bundle, he placed one hand against each side of the doorway and looked out to see if the 25-man ration box he had just kicked out was going to land in the camp spot. While he was looking out of the plane, the pilot hit a down draft and dropped several feet. The top of the doorway hit Richards on the back of his head at the base of his skull. He was slightly stunned and almost fell out of the door. He managed to push himself back away from the door and then sat down while the plane circled around for another pass. Feeling better, he got another bundle ready to kick out and they were able to drop the rest of the supplies in good shape. That was the last time he tried looking out to see if the cargo had dropped in the right place. It took two days to get all the material for the hundred-man camp dropped.

EARLY DAYS IN THE FOREST SERVICE, VOLUME 4, NORTHERN REGION

This hillside barbecue oven was constructed on a slope so that the front of the oven was the only evident part of the artificial construction. Side walls, roof, and floor was constructed of fire-clay brick with the floor being laid upon a reinforced concrete base. After the oven had been thoroughly heated, the ashes were raked from the oven before the meat was placed on the grill made of reinforced mesh. The front opening was closed with a double covering consisting of an inner shield of sheet iron which was locked in place during the actual cooking operation. The doors were then closed and locked with a small amount of earth placed against the bottom of the doors. When not in use, the main outside doors were kept fastened with a padlock.

BARBECUE PIT AT DEER CREEK CAMPGROUND, HUMBOLDT NATIONAL FOREST, NEVADA, JUNE 1940. (PHOTO BY P. S. BIELER)

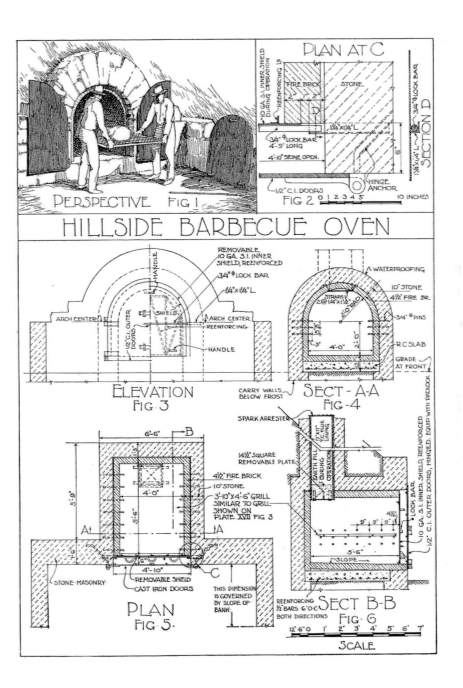

HILLSIDE BARBECUE OVEN

PERSPECTIVE FIG 1

PLAN AT C

FIG 2   0 1 2 3 4 5   10 INCHES

ELEVATION
FIG 3

SECT-A-A
FIG-4

PLAN
FIG 5.

SECT B-B
FIG 6

SCALE
12" 6" 0   1'   2'   3'   4'   5'   6'   7'

NEVER-FAIL PIT BARBECUE BRISKET

1 packet (1.06-ounce) McCormick mesquite dry marinade mix
1½ cup dark brown sugar (do not pack in cup
    when measuring, just pile lightly)
1 medium onion, sliced into rings
4- to 6-pound beef brisket (trim fat if needed)

In small bowl, combine spice packet and brown sugar. Set aside. Line Dutch oven with heavy duty aluminum foil (shiny side in), extending up and over sides of pan. Place onion slices in bottom of pan. Pat sugar/spice mixture onto brisket, with most of mixture on top of meat. Place brisket in Dutch oven and cover. Bury kettle in fire pit, piling hot coals on bottom, sides, and top of kettle. Cover with ashes or sod pad to keep in heat. Let sit 6–8 hours. Uncover. Remove meat carefully from kettle (will be very tender). Enjoy. Makes its own barbecue sauce as it cooks. Note: To make a "pit barbecue crust" form on meat, about 1 hour before eating, remove kettle from ground. Set in hot coals UNCOVERED.

This can also be cooked in an oven. If using an oven, be sure to use a deep heavy pan lined with foil. Extend foil sides up over pan, to protect oven from spattering. Heat oven to 275 degrees. Place prepared brisket in oven UNCOVERED for 6–8 hours. Tastes like it came right out of a campfire. Can cook all day while you're working and be ready when you come in to eat.

You can also use venison (shoulder or ham works well for this, deboned) instead of beef.

DAVID BUCK SEALS, REGION 10, TONGASS NATIONAL FOREST, ALASKA

TIP To impart a barbecue flavor to broiled meats, sprinkle with instant coffee while cooking.

SALMON POTATO CAMPFIRE BAKE

4 medium red potatoes, washed and sliced thinly
3 tablespoons flour
Salt and pepper to taste
1 cup smoked salmon, flaked (or use 1½ cups cooked, flaked salmon)
1 medium onion, chopped (or 3 green onions)
1 (10¾-ounce) can cream of mushroom soup (or cream of celery soup)
½ cup water
1 cup grated cheese (your choice of variety)

Place half of the potatoes in lightly greased Dutch oven (or line Dutch oven with aluminum foil, shiny side in, for easy cleanup). Sprinkle with half of flour, and salt and pepper. Cover with half of flaked salmon and onion. Repeat layers of potatoes, flour, spices, salmon, and onion. In bowl, combine soup and water, stirring until smooth. Pour over top of mixture. Do not stir. Sprinkle with cheese. Cover. Pile hot coals around sides and on top of kettle and cook for 40–45 minutes, or until potatoes are done (thinner potato slices cook faster).

If you want, add celery, asparagus, or peas to this. Can also be made with smoked ham instead of salmon. Makes 4 big servings.

David Buck Seals, Region 10, Tongass National Forest, Alaska

BRIDGER LAKE CAMPGROUND, WASATCH NATIONAL FOREST, 1959.

WILDERNESS RANGER FISH–COOKING METHOD

While I was a Wilderness Ranger on the Pasayten Wilderness and Pacific Crest National Scenic Trail on the Okanogan National Forest in Washington, I learned a handy way of cooking fish. Since I was back-packing in this seasonal Forest Service job, the method was a favorite of mine because I didn't carry a frying pan and cleanup did not involve dishes. Besides, I was in the presence of bears and lions and carried no cooking oil to serve as an attracting smell. I did bring fishing gear to catch these non-native, tasty fish.

INGREDIENTS AND NECESSARY EQUIPMENT:
• Fish, cleaned with the head attached
• Pointed narrow stick or other implement suitable
   for toasting marshmallows or hot dogs
• Fire

INSTRUCTIONS:
• Put the stick through the fish's mouth.
• Push the pointed end into the tail section of the fish,
   beginning at the posterior end of the body cavity.
• Toast as you would a hot dog until the fish is flaky and the eyes white.
• Cooking time: short

This method works best with fish less than 12 inches in length. Since properly cooked fish have flaky flesh, losing the fish into the fire is a very real possibility. With a little practice, you will soon get the hang of not rescuing your dinner from the fire. Hunger and the anticipation of eating fresh fish hastens the learning time.

JAMES E. STONE, REGION 4, REGIONAL OFFICE, UTAH

TIP

Eggs dipped in boiling water for 10 seconds will keep longer in a camp ice chest.

DUTCH OVEN CISCO (BEAR LAKE CISCO)

Put 2 to 3 cups lard (or shortening) in Dutch oven and preheat over coals until a drop of water splatters the melted lard. Place a mess of fresh or frozen cisco in Dutch oven and cook until crisp and brown. Scoop out, eat hot the entire fish—mountain man style. (Or if you like, you can clean and cut off the head of these smelt-like fish—but they are edible in their entirety.)

DON DUFF, REGION 4, RETIREE

FISHLAKE NATIONAL FOREST, UTAH, 1919.

ARTHUR J. WAGSTAFF scanned his faded diary pages from 1925 to recount memories on the Lemhi National Forest.

He recalled that after passing the Rangers' Exam, his offer of a job on the Lemhi required that he "furnish two horses and feed myself and horses for $110 per month." Home was Carey, Idaho, about 80 miles though the mountains to Mackay where he was to report. This meant a two-day trip over country with which he was not acquainted. He missed one trail and ended up near a place or ranch called Marten.

He wrote, "It was sundown and no place to put up for the night. I had no pack. Finally, I spotted a sheep camp a mile or two away. It turned out to be one of Brockies herds. There were two herders. They took me in, fed me, and we slept three in a bed. The next morning I took the road route for Mackay. I tried to cut through a wet meadow for a half mile to save about a mile and a half around the road, but it was too swampy. I arrived in Mackay that night."

OLD TIMERS NEWS, *INTERMOUNTAIN REGION*, OCTOBER 1979

MONTGOMERY M. "MONTY" ATWATER, WHO WORKED FOR THE FOREST SERVICE FROM 1946 THROUGH 1964, FINDS HIMSELF WITH MORE FISH THAN PAN. PHOTO COURTESY OF MONTGOMERY M. ATWATER II, WHO REMEMBERS HIS FATHER ALWAYS COMING BACK TO CAMP WITH THE LARGEST NUMBER OF FISH IN THE SHORTEST AMOUNT OF TIME.

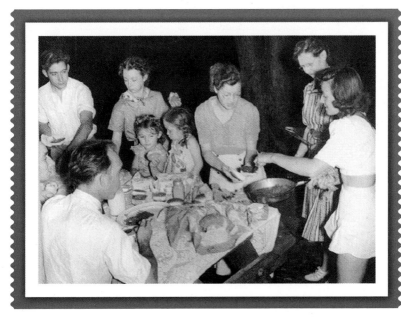

FROM FRYING PAN TO BUN: THE TALE OF A HAMBURGER. BREVORT LAKE CAMP AND PICNIC GROUND, REGION 9, MICHIGAN, MARQUETTE NATIONAL FOREST, MORAN RANGER DISTRICT, JULY 1939.

DUTCH OVEN SEAFOOD QUICHE

6 ounces shrimp or crabmeat
   (can be canned)
1 cup shredded cheddar cheese
3 ounces cream cheese
¼ cup diced green onions
12 ounces drained pimentos

2 cups milk
1 cup Bisquick baking mix
4 eggs
1 teaspoon salt
Dash of nutmeg

Thoroughly mix all ingredients together (use eggbeater or wire whip). Pour mixture into a 10- or 12-inch Dutch oven. Cover with coals and cook 50–55 minutes, or until knife inserted in quiche comes out clean and top is golden brown. Makes 6 to 8 servings.

MICHELLE HUFFMAN, REGION 4, ASHLEY NATIONAL FOREST, UTAH

JACK'S BEER-BATTERED TROUT (OR HALIBUT, OR ANY NICE FISH)

3 eggs
½ teaspoon each salt and pepper
½ bottle of beer
1 cup Bisquick baking mix

1 trout, skinned and filleted
3 cups cracker crumbs
Oil

Mix the eggs, salt and pepper, beer, and baking mix in a mixing bowl. Add enough beer to achieve a thick "pancake-like" batter. Dip the fish fillets in the batter and then roll them in the cracker crumbs. Fry the fish until golden brown in oil in a hot frying pan.

From Jack's guiding days in the Boundary Waters Canoe Area Wilderness. Jack Blackwell, Region 5, Regional Forester, California, retiree

Trout from Panguitch Lake, Utah, 1922.

GREAT BASIN RATTLESNAKE (DESERT WHITEFISH)

Clean and skin snake, cut off head (venom is confined to sacs in jaws). Cut rattlesnake into 2- to 3-inch sections. Grill over campfire coals, brush on butter. Grill until tender or "crispy critters"—your choice. Season with salt, pepper, and nutmeg. Or fry in buttered skillet until tender or browned. Add wild onion slices and/or dried sagebrush leaves—your choice or both.

DON DUFF, REGION 4, RETIREE

FIELD NOTE

In 1923, FRANCIS W. WOODS worked on the old Idaho National Forest (now the Payette) and told of adventures of a foot traverse down the Middle Fork of the Salmon River. The crew had been warned about an old timer who lived somewhere on the Middle Fork who had had some bad experiences with the law. They ran across this individual below the mouth of Big Creek, living in a small, one-room cabin. When they approached the house and looked inside, they noticed that he was busily cooking something in a large kettle. "Apparently he hadn't been cooking it very long as the mixture had not yet come to a boil. Above the stove there was a wooden shelf, and lying on it, a cat. As we entered the cabin and spoke to the man, he turned away from the stove and then turned back to his cooking. Seeing the cat, he took a swipe at it. He knocked it into the kettle! He then reached in, picked the cat up out of the mixture and when holding it above the kettle, ran his other hand down the dripping body of the cat to salvage what he could. Then he threw the cat out the door. We didn't stay with him very long and soon went about our business."

OLD TIMERS NEWS, *INTERMOUNTAIN REGION*, JUNE 1971

ELK RIBS OR BRISKET BARBECUE

3 to 4 pounds boneless elk
  brisket or elk ribs
3 to 4 tablespoons cooking oil
3 to 4 cloves garlic

2 medium onions
1 to 2 cups hearty Burgundy wine
6 to 8 cans beer
Barbecue sauce (optional)

Trim and pat dry brisket or ribs; cut into ½- to 1-pound chunks. Start 20 to 25 charcoal briquettes. When briquettes are well started, spread out half of them and set Dutch oven over them. Make sure the Dutch oven is level. Add cooking oil to Dutch oven and press garlic cloves into the oil as it warms. Sauté for 2–3 minutes. Add meat and turn frequently for a few minutes. Quarter or dice onions and arrange on top of meat. Leave 1 inch of space on top. Add wine and six-pack of beer (and barbecue sauce if you desire). Put lid on and add remaining briquettes to the lid. Be prepared to add more briquettes in about 1½ hours after starting. Check occasionally and add more beer if necessary. If you have any beer left, you can drink it while you wait.

BARBECUE SAUCE

2½ cups ketchup
½ cup prepared mustard
¾ cup brown sugar
1 tablespoon celery seed
1½ cups chili sauce
4 tablespoons Worcestershire sauce
1½ cups wine vinegar

2 tablespoons soy sauce
1½ cups water
2 cloves garlic, minced
¾ cup lemon juice
Dash of bottled hot pepper sauce
Ground black pepper to taste

Mix all ingredients together. Use as a marinade or cooking sauce.

DAN KRUTINA, REGION 4, RETIREE

McDUFF'S DUTCH OVEN ROAST—VENISON, ELK, OR MOOSE

Use 12- to 16-inch Dutch oven. Put 2 to 3 cups of lard (or shortening) or suet in oven and preheat in a healthy bed of coals. Preheat lid with coals too. Use 2- to 5-pound roast. Sear and brown roast in oven. Turn every 10–15 minutes. Salt and pepper. Options include use of garlic clove, sage, parsley, thyme, and nutmeg. Cook 20–30 minutes per pound or longer on medium coals. Keep coals covering entire lid of oven. When roast is about three-fourths cooked, add 2 to 6 sliced onions, 6 to 10 sectioned carrots, and 10 to 12 halved potatoes. Add more seasoning and one can beer (optional). Continue cooking until potatoes and carrots are tender and browned. Stir potatoes, onions, and carrots to bottom and around roast to brown. Serves 6 to 8 hungry river runners.

Don Duff, Region 4, retiree

Family picnic at Lake Vesuvius, Region 9, Wayne National Forest, Ironton Ranger District, Ohio, July 1952.

SHEPHERD'S PIE

1 pound bacon, cut into
  1-inch pieces
1 to 2 pounds ground beef
Instant mashed potatoes

2 (15-ounce) cans corn, drained
2 cans green beans, drained
Grated cheese of choice
Salt and pepper

Cook bacon, drain grease. Add ground beef and cook. While beef is cooking, prepare enough instant mashed potatoes (or real if you have the time/energy). When beef is completely cooked, add corn and green beans. Add a thick layer of mashed potatoes. Cover with 10 coals on lid and lower heat on bottom so meat does not burn. Let oven cook for 10 minutes, then top potatoes with grated cheese and cover until cheese melts. Season to taste with salt/pepper.

DAN KRUTINA, REGION 4, RETIREE

FIELD NOTE

FOREST SERVICE WIVES played a huge role in the early days of the agency and it was not until 1958 that Ranger Richard Leicht was allocated funds to hire a part-time clerk to work at the Altonah Ranger District. Until that time Leight's wife, Mary, helped out with district clerical duties. In an oral history conducted in 1984, she said, "A lot of the wives did a lot more than I did but I took my turn on the radio during fires. Also, many times when you were out on the forest, you were the only eating place. You fed whoever was there and if it was at midnight when the fire crews were getting ready to go, the coffee pot was on and they had the meals when they came in."

FROM RICHARD LEICHT ORAL HISTORY, REGION 4

BAKED DISH

1 small potato
½ pound ground round steak
1 small onion

1 stalk celery (if available)
½ (10.5-ounce) can tomato soup
Salt and pepper to taste

Alternate layers of potato, ground steak, onion, and celery until baking dish is filled. Pour tomato soup over top. Add salt and pepper. Grated cheese may be added on top if desired. Bake one hour at 350 degrees (moderate oven).

Bert E. Strom, Region 4, Boise National Forest, retiree

Recipe extracted from the U.S. Forest Service Region 6 Fire Control Lookout Cookbook, *dated June 1, 1943.*

Cooking on *a wood heater outdoors at job site on the* Chattahoochee National Forest in Georgia.

HUNTER'S LUNCH

1 small can mushrooms
½ onion, sliced
¼ pound ham in ½-inch strips
¼ pound bacon

½ cup cooked spaghetti
¼ cup canned tomatoes
½ (15-ounce) can lima beans
½ cup whole kernel corn

Fry together mushrooms, onion, ham, and bacon until done. Mix with all other ingredients and bake 30 minutes at 350 degrees (moderate oven).

BERT E. STROM, REGION 4, BOISE NATIONAL FOREST, RETIREE

RECIPE EXTRACTED FROM THE U.S. FOREST SERVICE REGION 6 FIRE CONTROL LOOKOUT COOKBOOK, DATED JUNE 1, 1943.

FIELD NOTE

J. W. "BILL" HUMPHREY wrote about his wife's involvement in district responsibilities on the Manti Forest Reserve in 1907 and 1908. Finding that being responsible for the ranger nursery required more time than he could give, his wife took over irrigating the young trees and keeping out the birds that were very destructive to the young plants. He said, "We lived 25 miles from the nearest town, over near impassable roads, with no neighbors or telephones, and save for an occasional homesick sheepherder, no visitors, so she was glad to find something to help pass the time. We had an iron roof on our one-room cabin for which, by the way, I was given an appropriation of $65 to build and furnish with a cook stove. And when it rained or hailed, which was quite often, the noise was so great you could not even hear it thunder. Those were the days—happy ones for all the family. We moved more than 25 times, to Orangeville, Logan, Moab, Panguitch, and Ephraim, in that order. I had to buy four homes and I only got my money back out of the last one I sold."

OLD TIMERS NEWS, INTERMOUNTAIN REGION, JUNE 1958

EASY TAMALE PIE

2 large cans of chili (your favorite brand)
1 jalapeño, chopped
1 can green chiles

1 package corn bread mix, prepared according to package directions

Mix chili, jalapeño, and green chiles and put in the bottom of a 12-inch Dutch oven. Cover this with prepared corn bread mix. Cook in oven with 8 briquettes on bottom and 15 briquettes on top. Cook 30 minutes or until corn bread is cooked through.

MARIAN JACKLIN, REGION 4, DIXIE NATIONAL FOREST, UTAH

MISS HELEN DOWE SAWS WOOD FOR THE CABIN STOVE AT THE DEVIL'S HEAD FIRE LOOKOUT, PIKE NATIONAL FOREST, COLORADO, 1919.

HAP AND
LUCILLE
WEST
JOHNSON

"The Ranger [Irwin H. "Hap" Johnson] also had his share of cooking. The several days to almost week-long pack trips over the Pine Valley Ranger District gave him considerable experience in this regard. On every pack trip the most important utensil was a small Dutch oven that he could use equally well over a campfire or when he stopped at either one of two guard stations where there was a small stove."

EXCERPT FROM MEMORIES OF A FOREST RANGER'S
WIFE BY LUCILLE WEST JOHNSON, 1987

SLOPPY JOE BISCUIT BAKE

1 medium onion, chopped
2 pounds lean ground beef
2 (1⅓-ounce) packages sloppy
  joe seasoning mix
2 (6-ounce) cans tomato paste
2 cups water
1 (16-ounce) package prepared
  refrigerator biscuits

Heat a 12-inch Dutch oven over 9 hot coals. Brown onion and ground beef. Add seasoning mix, tomato paste, and water, stirring well, and bring to a boil. Separate individual biscuits and place on top of the meat mixture. Cover with Dutch oven lid and place 15 hot coals on top. Cook, covered, for 15–20 minutes, or until biscuits are browned and cooked through. Serves 4 to 6.

DIAN THOMAS, FROM RECIPES FOR ROUGHING IT EASY

CUSTER CAMP, YANKEE FORK, CHALLIS NATIONAL FOREST, IDAHO, JULY 1937. (W. H. SHAFFER)

PIZZA

CRUST: 1-pound loaf of frozen bread dough, thawed

Divide dough in half. Roll each half into a circle and place in lightly greased Dutch ovens. Pat dough to fill Dutch oven and to make a raised edge to keep the toppings on the pizza.

SAUCE: Use your favorite premade pizza sauce

Spread ½ to ¾ cup sauce over dough. Then sprinkle with:

¼ teaspoon parsley flakes
½ teaspoon oregano

¼ cup grated Parmesan cheese
¼ pound grated mozzarella cheese

Top with your favorite pizza toppings like pepperoni, olives, ham, pineapple, precooked sausage or hamburger, onions, green peppers, mushrooms. One 1-pound loaf will make a 12- and a 14-inch pizza. For a 12-inch oven, use 18 briquettes on top and 12 on bottom. For a 14-inch oven, use 20 briquettes on top and 14 on bottom. Bake for 20–25 minutes.

BILLY KEITH, REGION 4, RETIREE

CCC *BOYS COOKING BOLOGNA SANDWICHES OVER A CAMPFIRE IN THE BLACK HILLS NATIONAL FOREST, SOUTH DAKOTA, 1940. BOYS WERE FROM CAMP F-6 LOCATED NEAR ROUBAIX, SOUTH DAKOTA. (PHOTO COURTESY NACCCA)*

FIRST NIGHT OUT PIZZA

One 10-inch frozen pizza and extra toppings to taste. Heat 12-inch Dutch oven to 450 degrees with 4 to 6 coals on bottom and 18 on top (more or less as needed). Put pizza in hot Dutch oven and cook as directed on package with additional time needed for thick extras. Retain the pizza box to use as insulated disposable plate.

ROBIN WIGNALL, REGION 8, DANIEL BOONE NATIONAL FOREST, KENTUCKY

FIELD NOTE

Your call for outdoor recipes got me thinking about my field days in Utah . . . I was the first Zone Archaeologist there and covered all of the Utah Forests including Ranger Districts in Colorado and Wyoming. I was on the road a lot. In fact, I would tell people that my job was "truck driver" since I practically lived in my Dodge pickup.

That ol' Dodge had a flat top and some manifold pipes created a couple of nice little places where I could stash a small can of beans, spaghetti, or whatnot. The cans would get hot, but never hot enough to explode, so it was a way to provide for a hot lunch out in the field. I often surprised some helper assigned for the day from a District by offering a "hot entree" to supplement their brown-bag lunch.

But the best fun came from going to a full-service gas station. Some poor mope would dive under the hood to check the oil. He'd pop up with an astonished look on his face and say, "There's spaghetti on your engine." "Oh, yeah," I'd say, "that's OK."

I never lost a can, even on the worst roads. But I would be less than frank if I claimed to have ever really enjoyed one of those lunches. Most of it really is "kid stuff" and they are welcome to it. I would not recommend any of it as "Heritage" cooking!

DAVID GULLIO, REGION 4, RETIREE

ENCHILADA PIE

2 pounds lean ground beef
1 medium onion, chopped
1 (11½-ounce) can condensed
   tomato soup
2 (10-ounce) cans mild or
   hot enchilada sauce

1 cup water
9 (8-inch) flour or corn tortillas
1½ to 2 cups (8 ounces) cheddar or
   Monterey Jack cheese, shredded

Heat a 12-inch Dutch oven over 9 hot coals. Brown meat and onion.
Pour off drippings. Add soup, enchilada sauce, and water and simmer
5 minutes. Spoon ⅔ of this mixture into a medium bowl, leaving remaining
⅓ in the Dutch oven. Arrange 2 to 3 tortillas over the meat mixture and
sprinkle with ⅓ of the cheese. Layer with half of the remaining meat
mixture and ⅓ of the cheese; repeat. Cover with Dutch oven lid and place
12 to 15 hot coals on top. Cook, covered, 10–15 minutes, or until cheese
melts and tortillas soften. Serves 6 to 8.

Dian Thomas, from Recipes for Roughing It Easy

L. O. Peck, Ranger,
cooking on stove
set up during
overnight stop
at Spanish Lake,
Spanish Peaks
Wilderness,
Gallatin National
Forest, Montana,
August 1955. (Photo
by W. E. Steuerwald)

DESSERTS

EASY PEACH DUTCH OVEN COBBLER

2 cans sliced peaches, drained
1 yellow cake mix

1 (12-ounce) can lemon-lime soda

Put drained peaches in the bottom of a 12-inch Dutch oven. Sprinkle the cake mix over the peaches, then pour the soda over the top of it. Stir the mix completely. With the lid on, bake for 45–60 minutes using 12 briquettes on the top and 12 briquettes on the bottom. Rotate the oven and lid every 15 minutes. Serve warm with ice cream. Serves 8 to 10 people.

JOHN HOEL, REGION 4, REGIONAL OFFICE, RETIREE

ELK CREEK RANGER STATION, BOISE NATIONAL FOREST, IDAHO, 1939. (PHOTO BY P. S. BIELER)

FRED W. CLEATOR, MRS. GROVER BURCH, AND VALIDA ROBINSON
AT SPECTACLE MEADOWS CAMP CLEANING CAMP POTS AND PANS,
DESCHUTES NATIONAL FOREST, OREGON, 1940.

CHERRY COBBLER

2 large cans of cherry pie filling
1 package sour cream cake mix

1 (12-ounce) can lemon-lime soda

Line the bottom of 12-inch Dutch oven with foil. Pour in the cans of cherry pie filling and cover with dry cake mix. Pour ¾ can of lemon-lime soda over the cake mix and put the lid on. Place 8 briquettes on bottom and 15 briquettes on top. Cook for 35–40 minutes. Check at 30 minutes to see if you need to take off the bottom coals and put fresh ones on top. Cake should be browned. Serve with ice cream or real whipped cream.

MARIAN JACKLIN, REGION 4, DIXIE NATIONAL FOREST, UTAH

Mirror Lake Campground, early 1930s, Wasatch National Forest, Utah.

DUTCH OVEN COBBLER

2 large cans fruit pie filling
1 cake mix
Ingredients on box

Vanilla ice cream or
    whipped topping

Line Dutch oven with aluminum foil. Spread pie filling in bottom of Dutch oven. Mix cake according to directions on box. Spread over fruit. Cook in Dutch oven for 35–45 minutes (cook using briquettes on top and bottom—about 16 briquettes in total). Try these combinations: chocolate cake/cherry, white cake/raspberry or blueberry, yellow cake/apple. Top with vanilla ice cream or whipped topping.

Nancy Murray, Region 4, former employee

DUTCH OVEN FRUIT COBBLER

Preheat Dutch oven. Use a white or yellow cake mix that needs oil, eggs, and water. Mix as directed on package. Put ½ cube butter (or margarine) in bottom of 12-inch Dutch oven and place over fire until butter melts. Pour in pie filling mix (cherry, apple, blueberry, or your own favorite pie filling mix). Spread mix around to cover bottom of Dutch oven. Pour prepared cake batter over top of filling—be sure pie filling is completely covered with batter. Place lid on Dutch oven and bake for 10–20 minutes on top of hot coals. Place some of the hot coals on top of the lid. Check to see if cake is done and if not, bake a few more minutes.

If you are on a camping trip, an alternative to mixing in a bowl is to place all ingredients of cake mix in two plastic bags, one inside the other. Release all air and put a twist tie on top of each bag to seal them. Knead the batter with your fingers until cake mix is thoroughly mixed. Pour over pie filling in Dutch oven and cook.

VAUGHN FRANCIS, REGION 4, RETIREE

HIKERS CAMPING OVERNIGHT AT ONE OF 12 SHELTERS ON APPALACHIAN TRAIL, NANTAHALA NATIONAL FOREST, NORTH CAROLINA, BETWEEN THE CHATTAHOOCHEE NATIONAL FOREST (GEORGIA) AND GREAT SMOKY MOUNTAINS NATIONAL PARK, JULY 1960.

CARAMEL APPLE COBBLER

3 cans of apple pie filling
1 package caramel cake mix (Duncan Hines makes this flavor)
1 (12-ounce) can of lemon-lime soda

Line the bottom of a 12-inch Dutch oven with foil. Pour in the cans of apple pie filling and cover with dry cake mix. Pour ¾ can of lemon-lime soda over the cake mix and put the lid on. Place 8 briquettes on the bottom and 15 briquettes on top. Cook 35–40 minutes. Check at 30 minutes to see if you need to take off the bottom coals and put fresh ones on top. Cake should be browned. Serve with ice cream or real whipped cream.

MARIAN JACKLIN, REGION 4, DIXIE NATIONAL FOREST, UTAH

WASATCH NATIONAL FOREST, UTAH, CIRCA 1940.

ZIGZAG RIVER, UMPQUA NATIONAL FOREST, OREGON.

FIELD NOTE

In the spring of 1918, the phone rang at the old mining camp building at the mouth of Deadwood River, Boise National Forest, and EARL TEMPLETON, one of the men working on a road crew assigned to the Garden Valley–Lowman Road, was called to the phone. The clerk in the Boise office stated there was a telegram from Marion, Iowa, saying a daughter had been born to Earl the day before and both baby and mother were doing fine. Templeton wrote, "In about half an hour, the phone rang again, and the deputy supervisor read the telegram to me. He did not know that the clerk had delivered the message. The crew joked then, saying no doubt it was twins. I left camp June 15, went to Jerome to check on the condition of my horses, then on east to get my wife and baby."

OLD TIMERS NEWS, INTERMOUNTAIN REGION, FEBRUARY 1967

APPLE CRUNCH

¼ cup (½ stick) butter or margarine
½ cup brown sugar
¼ teaspoon cinnamon
¼ teaspoon nutmeg

6 cooking apples, peeled,
   cored, and sliced
2 cups sugar cookie crumbs

Heat a 12-inch Dutch oven over 12 hot coals; melt butter and stir in sugar, cinnamon, and nutmeg, and cook, stirring frequently, until sugar dissolves and a syrup forms. Cook apples in the syrup for 10–20 minutes, or until apples are soft. Top with cookie crumbs and serve hot or cold. Serves 6. (You may want to line the Dutch oven with heavy-duty aluminum foil before cooking for easy cleanup.)

DIAN THOMAS, FROM RECIPES FOR ROUGHING IT EASY

SYD TREMEWAN AND ARCHIE BELL AT THE HUMBOLDT NATIONAL FOREST SUPERVISOR'S OFFICE (GOLD CREEK RANGER STATION), NEVADA, 1913.

Former Supervisor DAN PACK told of office conditions in the early days. He said, "A lot of Supervisors' offices were on some back street where rent was low. If a Supervisor rented an up-to-date office in a good location, at the end of the month, after paying his office rent, he wouldn't have enough left to buy a hot-dog. Many Supervisors' offices in those days were a one-room affair. The furniture consisted of about three chairs, a small table and a makeshift filing system. Not many offices had a typewriter. If a Forest Service officer desired a copy of some important letter it was up to him to turn to the old letter press." In 1908, when Pack was working in the Washington office, he heard that the "grand old-timer, Mr. Pinchot, was devoting a large portion of his time to forestry for a grand total of one-dollar per year and the love he had to see the trees and the grasses grow."

OLD TIMERS NEWS, *INTERMOUNTAIN REGION, MARCH 1954*

MIXED BERRY CRISP

1 (10-ounce) bag frozen
  raspberries, thawed
1 (10-ounce) bag frozen
  blueberries, thawed

1 (10-ounce) bag frozen
  boysenberries or
  blackberries, thawed
¾ cup sugar

In a bowl combine berries and sugar; set aside. Prepare crisp topping.

CRISP TOPPING:
1 cup all-purpose flour
1 cup walnuts, finely chopped
1 cup brown sugar

1 cup oats
½ cup (1 stick) butter or
  margarine, melted

Mix all topping ingredients in a medium bowl or in a 1-quart resealable plastic bag.

Heat a 12-inch Dutch oven over 9 hot coals. Cover with Dutch oven lid and place 15 hot coals on the top. Preheat 10 minutes. Pour the berry mixture into the Dutch oven. Sprinkle crisp topping mix evenly onto berries. Bake covered, for 30–35 minutes. Serve warm or cold. Serves 6 to 8.

DIAN THOMAS, FROM RECIPES FOR ROUGHING IT EASY

FIELD NOTE

GEORGE C. LARSON recalled that he was one of only five rangers in the region in 1915. He said, "Crude is a very charitable word to use for the ranger stations we were to occupy. I remember rejoicing when we were granted a 75 cent per diem if we were away from the station more than 24 hours." He recalled Ranger Jensen on the Fillmore District constructing a toilet at his summer station, cutting two holes in the seat, one large and one small. Over the small hole, he placed a sign saying, "For Rangers 75 cents per diem," and over the larger, "For Supervisors, $2.00 per diem."

OLD TIMERS NEWS, INTERMOUNTAIN REGION, FEBRUARY 1967

CARROT PUDDING

2 cups flour
1 cup sugar
1½ teaspoons baking soda
½ teaspoon cloves
½ teaspoon allspice
½ teaspoon nutmeg

1 teaspoon cinnamon
1 teaspoon salt
1 cup carrots, grated
1 cup potatoes, grated
½ cup shortening
1 cup raisins

Mix together first 8 ingredients. Add carrots and potatoes and mix. Mix in shortening. Add raisins. Mix all well. Put in wide mouth jars—about 3 jars. Poke 1 to 2 holes in top of jar lid. Hot bathe them just to neck of jar. Cook 3 hours in boiling bath. Can be frozen.

ALDA DOPP

MISS HELEN DOWE IN DEVIL'S HEAD LOOKOUT TOWER USING THE OSBORNE FIREFINDER, PIKE NATIONAL FOREST, COLORADO, 1919.

DEVIL'S HEAD FIRE LOOKOUT, PIKE NATIONAL FOREST, COLORADO, SHOWING GLASSED-IN OBSERVATORY AND LOOKOUT, MISS HELEN DOWE, JULY 1919.

CRAISIN BREAD PUDDING

6 eggs
½ cup sugar
½ cup sour cream
1 cup half-and-half or milk
½ loaf bread

½ cup craisins or raisins
½ cup walnuts, chopped
¾ cup brown sugar
½ cup (1 stick) butter or
    margarine, melted

In a small mixing bowl, mix together eggs, sugar, sour cream, and half-and-half. Line a 12-inch Dutch oven with heavy-duty aluminum foil. Layer ingredients in this order: ½ of the bread, craisins or raisins, walnuts, premixed liquids, brown sugar, and butter or margarine. Repeat in the same order using remaining ingredients.

Heat Dutch oven over 9 hot coals. Cover with Dutch oven lid and place 15 hot coals on the top, creating a 325-degree oven. Bake, covered, 30–40 minutes, or until a toothpick inserted in the center comes out clean. Serve warm. Serves 6 to 8.

DIAN THOMAS, FROM RECIPES FOR ROUGHING IT EASY

PIÑA COLADA CAKE DESSERT

1 (20-ounce) can crushed
   pineapple with juice
1 white cake mix

1 cup butter, melted
1 cup chopped almonds
1 cup shredded coconut

Pour the pineapple and juice into a 12-inch Dutch oven that has been lined with foil and sprayed with nonstick spray. Sprinkle cake mix over top of pineapple. Pour melted butter over the cake mix. Sprinkle on the nuts and then the coconut. Bake for about 55 minutes with 6 to 8 coals on the bottom (arranged in a circle around the outside edge) and 12 to 16 coals on top (arranged in two concentric circles).

MIKE AND CHERYL YASUDA, REGION 4, CARIBOU-TARGHEE NATIONAL FOREST, PALISADES RANGER DISTRICT, IDAHO

DOING DISHES AT SOAPSTONE CAMPGROUND, WASATCH NATIONAL FOREST, UTAH, 1933.

EASY OPEN FIRE CAKE DESSERT

2 cups flour
¼ cup sugar
½ teaspoon cinnamon
1 teaspoon baking powder
1 egg

½ cup water
3 fresh apples, chopped up very
    small and covered with sugar
    (other fruit can be substituted)

Mix flour, sugar, cinnamon, and baking powder together. Add egg and water. Place mixture in hand-greased Dutch oven. Add apples over top of mix. Cover and place to side of coals. Keep turning oven slowly to bake evenly. Great dessert.

TERRI VINING, REGION 8, OZARK-ST. FRANCIS
NATIONAL FORESTS, ARKANSAS, RETIREE

LONG DAYS AND
OVERNIGHTS WERE
AN ACCEPTED
PART OF THE
JOB, WASATCH
NATIONAL FOREST,
UTAH, 1914.

20-STEP CANNED CAKE

1. Have your wide-mouth half-pint canning jars, lids, and flats cleaned and ready.

2. Mix up any cake mix as per the instructions on the box.

3. Mix in something like M&M's candy or chocolate chips to give the bottom part of the cake something extra.

4. Mix up a "gooey and sticky" icing—something that will seep down into the cake a short way.

5. Only fill the half-pint jars about one-fourth to one-third full; the cake will rise as it bakes.

6. Place jars in a 350-degree oven on cookie sheets for 20–25 minutes. It takes a little longer due to the glass canning jar.

7. Test the cake with a toothpick.

8. Remove the cakes from the oven and add the icing.

9. Poke the cake with a chopstick to allow the icing to seep into the cake.

10. If the cake raised above the lip of the jar, just take a knife and trim the top, leaving room for the icing.

11. Carefully wipe the jar rims with a damp cloth to have them as clean as possible. Watch out, they are hot.

12. Place a flat and lid on each jar; tighten them by hand. Watch out again, they are still hot.

13. Turn them upside down on a layer of towels on your countertop.

14. Allow the jars to cool. You will hear the jars seal.

15. When cool, turn the jars over and test the flats for sealing.

16. If any did not seal, set those aside. They are what you get after dinner.

17. If they all sealed, set one aside and place the rest on a shelf for storage.

18. Boil some water.

19. Clean up the kitchen, put away all of your pots and pans.

20. Make a cup of tea, get a good book, sit in a comfy chair, and sample your cake.

Dan Krutina, Region 4, retiree

CHOCOLATE LOVER'S DELIGHT

1½ cups water
¼ cup cocoa powder
1 cup brown sugar
1 (10-ounce) bag miniature
   marshmallows

1 chocolate cake mix
   (prepared as directed)
6 ounces chocolate chips

Line the bottom and sides of a 12-inch Dutch oven with heavy foil. Mix the water, cocoa powder, and brown sugar together and pour into the Dutch oven. Add marshmallows and spread them out evenly. Pour prepared chocolate cake mix over marshmallows. Sprinkle chocolate chips over cake batter. Cover oven and bake using 8 to 10 briquettes on bottom and 14 to 16 briquettes on top for 60 minutes. Serve warm. Serves 10 to 12.

SUSAN MCDANIEL, REGION 4, REGIONAL OFFICE, UTAH

CAMPERS AT WARM LAKE CAMPGROUND, PAYETTE NATIONAL FOREST, IDAHO, 1939.

FIRE CAMP MESS LINE AT CAMP #5, SELWAY FALLS FIRE, KANIKSU NATIONAL FOREST, IDAHO, AUGUST 1934. (PHOTO BY K. D. SWAN)

FIELD NOTE

Pack rats were, unfortunately, a part of early-day cabin life. SAM BILLINGS wrote about being a part of a cruising party that cruised the burned timber following the big fires in 1926 on the old Kaniksu National Forest. He recalled:

"We camped in a cabin up in the burn in Harvey Creek. By some miracle the cabin hadn't burned although fire had burned within a few feet of it all the way around. . . . The cabin had a dirt roof and some of the crew said there were so many pack rats in the cabin it couldn't burn. Art Bowman had a Colt .22 automatic and shot pack rats every evening for a while after we had gone to bed and the gas lantern was turned out. The rats would come out almost immediately and someone would point them out with his flashlight and Art would shoot them.

"The camp cook did his cooking under a tarp that was stretched and fastened to the front of the cabin. He had a little mix-up table directly under the glassless window at the front of the cabin. One evening, as usual, a pack rat was heard scrambling around, someone turned his flashlight on it just as it went through the window onto the mix-up table and Art took a quick shot at it. He missed the rat but he sure didn't miss the three nested aluminum kettles that were on the table. The cook was fit to be tied."

EARLY DAYS IN THE FOREST SERVICE, VOLUME 4, NORTHERN REGION

CHERRY CHOCOLATE FUDGE CAKE

2 (21-ounce) cans cherry pie filling
1 (1 pound 2¼-ounce) package chocolate fudge cake
   mix (prepared according to package directions)

Pour pie filling into bottom of a large (12-inch) Dutch oven. Gently pour the prepared cake mix over the cherries. Cover and cook 45–60 minutes—test with toothpick. Do not overcook on the bottom.

BILL LEVERE, REGION 4, REGIONAL OFFICE, UTAH, RETIREE

TIP

If the oven has no gauge to tell the temperature, put either a slice of bread or white paper in the oven. If it turns brown quickly, the oven is too hot for most things. If it turns brown in about 5 minutes, you have a moderate oven.

A SNUG DEER HUNTERS' CAMP IN BEAVER CANYON, FISHLAKE NATIONAL FOREST, UTAH, 1938. (PHOTO BY F. C. KOZIOL)

STATE GAME WARDEN AT WARM SPRINGS RANGER STATION, BOISE NATIONAL FOREST, IDAHO, AUGUST 1930.

FIELD NOTE

ELSIE GODDEN remembered her years as a Ranger's wife on the Lemhi Ranger Station, Salmon National Forest, Idaho, in her letter published in the *Old Timers News* of June 1979. She recalled that in April of 1929, her travels took her to Hayden Creek where "a sweet old couple had a lovely old house with rag rugs and comfortable, well-worn furniture. It was a pleasure to get there in time for the noon meal. She was a good cook, and my cooking wasn't so hot. One day we stopped, and I went to the kitchen to help her. She was frying 'chicken.' She said, 'Now remember that this is chicken.' I promised that I wouldn't say a word. The hired man had shot grouse the day before the season opened, and the Forest Ranger was also the game warden at that time. While we were enjoying the fried chicken, the hired man said, 'Has anyone seen the Forest Ranger lately?' Another said, 'You are sitting beside him.' There was a dead silence, and he looked very embarrassed, but the matter was not referred to again. Hospitality means a great deal."

WAR CAKE

2 cups brown sugar
4 tablespoons shortening
1 cup raisins
½ teaspoon cloves
2 cup hot water
1 teaspoon salt

1 teaspoon cinnamon
3 cups flour
1 heaping tablespoon cocoa
1 teaspoon baking powder
1 teaspoon baking soda, dissolved
1 cup walnuts

Cook together for a few minutes the first seven ingredients. Cool. When cold or nearly so, add the next four ingredients with the baking soda dissolved in 1 tablespoon hot water. Add nuts. Bake at 350 degrees for 30 minutes. Can be frosted with a cream cheese frosting or boiled coconut/nut frosting.

MARY ELLEN BOSWORTH, MOTHER OF CHIEF DALE BOSWORTH

TROUBLE FOR THIS PACK STRING OCCURRED WHEN A FIDGETY HORSE ACTED UP IN THE MIDDLE OF THE GREYS RIVER ON THE OLD WYOMING NATIONAL FOREST, WYOMING. BARRUS (GUARD) ON HORSE AND SHUMWAY (COOK) IN WATER AFTER BEING DRAGGED FROM HIS HORSE BY THE LEAD ROPE OF THE SECOND PACK HORSE.

CANYON CAKE

Here is the recipe for what is known by all of Morris Gibbs's descendants as Canyon Cake:

3 cups water
2 cups sugar
½ pound raisins (approx. 2 ½ cups)

3 heaping tablespoons lard
(other types of shortening
do not work as well)

Combine the water, sugar, and raisins in a large pot on the stove. Boil together for 5 minutes or until raisins are soft. Remove from heat and add the lard. While the mixture is cooling combine the following:

3 cups all-purpose flour
1 teaspoon ground cinnamon
1 teaspoon baking soda
1 teaspoon ground cloves

1 teaspoon salt
½ teaspoon ground nutmeg
4 teaspoons cocoa (more if desired)

Combine dry ingredients and add them to cooled raisin mixture in the pan. Mix well. Pour into greased, floured 9 x 13 cake pan. Bake in 350-degree oven for approximately 1 hour (until toothpick in center comes out clean). Serve with or without frosting.

VAL R. GIBBS, RETIREE, SAFFORD, ARIZONA

NOTE FROM VAL: This cake went to the mountains of the Cache, Humboldt, Salmon, Challis, Sawtooth, and Targhee Forests and always was appreciated as the dessert after meals prepared over an open fire. This cake could be carried or packed and still remain intact and very tasty even after several days of riding over rough terrain.

This "butterless, milkless, eggless cake" was acquired by the new bride of E. Morris Gibbs soon after their marriage in 1918. Morris was an employee at that time on the old Cache Forest at Logan, Utah. He later worked on the Salmon Forest and then back to the Cache Forest where he retired.

This recipe was passed down to his son, Val R. Gibbs, who worked thirty-one years on the above forests and used this cake on all of them in his extensive packing into the backcountry. It would be nice to know the miles this cake traveled on the back of a horse!

PINEAPPLE UPSIDE-DOWN CAKE

2 tablespoons butter or
  margarine, melted
1 (16-ounce) can pineapple
  slices, drained
1 (8-ounce) jar maraschino cherries

½ cup brown sugar
1 (18¼-ounce) box yellow cake
  mix, prepared according
  to package directions

Line the bottom of a 12-inch Dutch oven with heavy-duty aluminum foil. Add butter or margarine and arrange pineapple slices on top. Set a maraschino cherry in the center of each pineapple slice, and sprinkle brown sugar evenly over the fruit. Pour prepared cake batter on top of the fruit.

Place the Dutch oven over 9 hot coals. Cover with Dutch oven lid and place 15 hot coals on top. Bake, covered, for 30 minutes, or until golden brown and a toothpick inserted in the center comes out clean.

Lift the cake out of the Dutch oven using the aluminum foil lining and set it on the table. Cover the top with aluminum foil, and tuck the edges underneath the cake. Cool for 10 minutes; turn upside down and peel away the foil. Serves 10 to 12.

Dian Thomas, from Recipes for Roughing It Easy

Hot lunch time for CCC boys at Happy Camp ECW Camp F-21, Happy Camp, California, 1933.

COCONUT PINEAPPLE CAKE

CAKE:
2 cups flour
2 teaspoons salt
2 teaspoons baking powder
5 eggs
¾ cup sugar
2 teaspoons vanilla extract
⅓ cup oil
Milk (to desired consistency)

TOPPING:
1 (13.5-ounce) can coconut milk
1 (20-ounce) can crushed pineapple
1 can sweetened condensed milk
⅓ cup regular milk
1 (8-ounce) package coconut
1 (8-ounce) package walnuts

Mix flour, salt, and baking powder. Set aside. Cream eggs and sugar. Then add vanilla and oil. Add ⅓ of flour mixture. Mix. Add ½ cup of milk. Mix. Add rest of flour mixture. Mix. Add rest of milk. Mix. Bake like any cake. This can be made on top of stove, in a Dutch oven, or in the embers.

For topping, mix coconut milk and pineapple. In a separate container mix condensed milk with regular milk. While cake is still hot, punch many holes all over it with a fork, then pour pineapple and coconut mixture over cake slowly. With egg turner, lift up cake around edges and pour liquid underneath also. Do the same with milk mixture. Sprinkle coconut and walnuts (broken) on top. Good? Yes, indeed! Fattening? Ooooohhhh, nooooo!!! Ha!!!

Myrl Ann Gutierrez, Region 4, Humboldt-Toiyabe National Forest, Nevada

FIELD NOTE

From 1950: Regional Forester C. J. OLSEN said that a few National Forest campgrounds in the Intermountain Region will continue to make "small use charges" on an experimental basis during the summer of 1950. Picnickers will pay 50 cents for a party of six; campers will pay 50 cents a day or $3 a week for the same size party.

Old Timers News, *Intermountain Region, June 1970*

COFFEE CAKE

½ cup (1 stick) butter or
   margarine, lightly melted
1 cup (8 ounces) sour cream
½ cup sugar
4 eggs, beaten
1 (18¼-ounce) box yellow cake mix

½ cup brown sugar
2 tablespoons cinnamon
1 cup walnuts, finely chopped
½ cup dried apricots,
   finely chopped
Vegetable oil as needed

In a 1-gallon plastic resealable bag, add butter or margarine, sour cream, and sugar; push out air and seal. Squeeze to mix; add eggs and squeeze well. Add dry cake mix and squeeze batter 2–3 minutes.

In a 1-quart plastic resealable bag, mix together brown sugar, cinnamon, walnuts, and apricots.

Line a 12-inch Dutch oven with heavy-duty aluminum foil and heat over 9 hot coals. Cover with Dutch oven lid and place 15 hot coals on the top. Preheat for 10 minutes. Lightly oil foil and pour half of the batter into the Dutch oven. Sprinkle with half of the topping; add remaining batter and sprinkle with the remaining topping. Cook, covered, for 40–50 minutes, or until a toothpick inserted into the center comes out clean. Cool 10–15 minutes. Lift out foil to serve. Serves 8 to 10.

DIAN THOMAS, FROM RECIPES FOR ROUGHING IT EASY

DOUBLE OVEN,
CIRCA 1950.

STRAWBERRY SHORTCAKE

2 cups flour
½ cup sugar
3 teaspoons baking powder
1½ sticks margarine, softened

1 egg, beaten
¼ to ⅓ cup water
2 pounds strawberries
¼ to ½ cup sugar

(Temperature: Equivalent of 325 degrees to 350 degrees)

In a large mixing bowl, combine flour, sugar, and baking powder. Add margarine and cut it into the mixture with a fork or pastry cutter. Work with it as little as possible—leave margarine in chunks. Stir in the egg and enough water to make a sticky dough. Do not overmix. Transfer the dough into a medium (10-inch) Dutch oven that has been lightly dusted with flour. Bake for 30–45 minutes or until top is lightly browned. Wash and cut strawberries in half, and mix with sugar in bowl. Serve shortcake with strawberries on top. Also good with milk poured on top.

BILL LEVERE, REGION 4, REGIONAL OFFICE, UTAH, RETIREE

FIELD NOTE

ROY WHITMORE was closing the Larson Creek smoke chaser station when Robert G. Elliott arrived to help out in the fall of 1924. Roy knew Elliott was on his way and greeted him by saying, "The ranger told me you would be down today. I have a treat before I cook supper." The treat was a crockery jug of homemade wine. He said, "I've been practicing all summer long, and this is my best product—I made it from the dried and canned fruit the Forest Station furnishes us, plus the sugar and a cake of yeast and, now in the fall, some huckleberries." Elliott acknowledged that it was delicious. Also powerful.

EARLY DAYS IN THE FOREST SERVICE,
VOLUME 4, NORTHERN REGION

FIELD NOTE

Northern Region's W. K. "BILL" SAMSEL wrote about early-day lookouts when structures did not exist.

Living quarters were primitive and the Forest Service "furnished a tent, a few cooking utensils, and a bed, consisting of 3 OD army type wool blankets and a tarp, a double bitted axe and fire tools. It was up to the man to use his own ingenuity and skill as a woodsman in making his quarters as comfortable as possible.

"Since the Forest Service did not furnish a stove we built a rock fireplace where we did the fry cooking and boiling, then an oven in the rocks for baking bread. This done, our quarters were complete, still quite primitive but we managed to get along and be quite comfortable most of the time. It has been said before and I am sure it is true, that it took a special breed of men to fill these jobs and live under such primitive conditions. They had to love the mountains and be possessed of the old pioneer spirit. Starting wages for a first-year lookout man was $70 per month, including board and room. And, at first, room was 'all the outdoors.'

"Because all food had to be packed in by mule train, which took from 4 to 6 days from the road end, and because there were no facilities for keeping fresh foods, they had to be of a non-perishable nature. A typical grub list would run about as follows: flour, baking powder, salt, sugar, coffee, beans, rice, dried apricots, prunes, and raisins. Sometimes there were dehydrated potatoes. For meat there was ham and bacon, and sometimes a little canned corned beef. Other canned foods consisted of corn, tomatoes, milk, and syrup. Some years later when the Forest Service began to furnish canned fruit and apple butter we thought this was really high living. It is only fair to say that we supplemented our diet with huckleberries and fish when we were able to get to where they were. Also when grouse season opened that helped, too."

EARLY DAYS IN THE FOREST SERVICE, VOLUME 4, NORTHERN REGION

TASTY CAMPFIRE APPLES IN TINFOIL

3 to 4 apples
1 cube butter, melted

½ cup maple syrup
1 cup chopped walnuts

Peel and cut apples into slices, taking out the core. Combine the melted butter, maple syrup, and nuts in a bowl. Place a small handful of apples onto a piece of aluminum foil. Top the apples with a large spoonful of the nut mixture. Fold the foil, leaving an opening for ventilation. Place on the campfire and cook 30–40 minutes, or until the apples are soft but not mushy.

Janet Thorsted, Region 4, Regional Office, Utah

Salmon National Forest lookout, Idaho, 1925.

DUTCH OVEN APPLE PIE

1 package premade pie crusts
  (let's make this easy)
5 cups apples, peeled and sliced
⅔ cup sugar
2 tablespoons flour

½ teaspoon cinnamon
Sprinkle of salt
2 tablespoons margarine
1 tablespoon sugar

(Temperature: Equivalent of 375 degrees to 400 degrees)

If you want to make this easy, get a pie tin that fits down in the bottom of your Dutch oven—a medium (10-inch) or a large (12-inch). If you don't have one, don't worry. Just follow these instructions, but do them directly in the bottom of your Dutch oven. However, I recommend dusting the bottom of the Dutch oven with a bit of flour before you put the pie crust in it. Put the first pie crust in the bottom of the pie tin and up the sides. In a separate bowl, mix the apples, sugar, flour, cinnamon, and salt. Pour this mixture into the first crust. Dot mixture with the margarine. Take the second pie crust from the package and cut it into ½-inch strips. Put the strips about ½ inch apart over the top of the pie in one direction first and then the opposite direction (again ½ inch apart), forming a lattice appearance. Push the edges of the top pie crust into the bottom pie crust so that they stick together, and then cut away any extra. Sprinkle the top with the remaining sugar. Cover and bake 45 minutes to 1 hour.

BILL LEVERE, REGION 4, REGIONAL OFFICE, UTAH, RETIREE

FIELD NOTE

JIM ADCOCK, one of the old Selway gang, was doing his best to cobble up a meal for a half-dozen hungry, unexpected visitors, from the inadequacies of a late-in-the-season, two-man camp. Jim had a deep bass voice, a Southern accent, and a slow, hesitant method of delivery. When he stuck his head out the door, the expectantly waiting men started to rise, but instead of the usual "Come and get it!" they heard him say, "If you don't like soup . . . supper's over."

EARLY DAYS IN THE FOREST SERVICE, VOLUME 4, NORTHERN REGION

CREAMY PUMPKIN PIE

¼ teaspoon salt
1½ cups whole wheat flour
2 tablespoons oil
½ cup cold water
1 (15-ounce) can pumpkin
2 eggs

1 (16-ounce) can sweetened
   condensed milk
¼ teaspoon pumpkin pie spice
½ teaspoon nutmeg
¼ teaspoon cinnamon
½ pint heavy cream
2 tablespoons honey

Stir salt into flour. Mix in oil using a fork. Add water, a few drops at a time, until dough holds together easily. Place in bottom of a heated, well-seasoned, 8-inch Dutch oven. Combine pumpkin with eggs, half the milk, and spices. Pour into shell. Bake 1 hour with 4 briquettes underneath and 9 on top for medium oven. Whip cream until thick, adding honey as cream begins to stiffen. Serve pie topped with whipped cream.

T. M. Leonard, Region 4, Ashley National Forest, retiree

Ranger at overnight trail camp, Taylor Lake, Deschutes National Forest, Oregon.

BACKPACKING BARS

¾ cup flour
½ cup quick-cooking oats
½ cup butter, softened
¼ cup toasted wheat germ
1 tablespoon grated orange peel

¾ cup brown sugar, divided
2 eggs
1 (4½-ounce) can blanched
  whole almonds
½ cup shredded coconut

Preheat oven to 350 degrees. Mix first 5 ingredients with ½ cup brown sugar until just mixed. At medium speed, beat 2 minutes (mixture will look dry). With lightly floured hands, pat into 8 x 8-inch baking dish. In a small bowl mix eggs with remaining ¼ cup brown sugar. Stir in almonds and coconut. Spread over mixture. Bake for 35 minutes.

MARY MCDONOUGH, ROCKY MOUNTAIN RESEARCH STATION, COLORADO

CAMPERS AT SUTTLE LAKE, DESCHUTES NATIONAL FOREST, OREGON, AUGUST 1936.

SHAKE AND MAKE ICE CREAM

YOU WILL NEED:
1 gallon-size heavy plastic resealable bag (not the slide-lock kind)
Ice (you can use ice cubes, crushed ice, or snow, it doesn't matter)
6 tablespoons rock salt (it must be rock salt, not table salt)

FOR THE ICE CREAM:
2 tablespoons white granulated sugar
1 cup milk (use either whole or 2% milk)
½ teaspoon vanilla
One pint-size heavy plastic resealable bag (not the slide-lock kind)

TO MAKE THE ICE CREAM: Fill the big bag a little less than half full of ice. Add the rock salt. Set aside for a moment. In the little bag, put the sugar, milk, and flavorings. Seal the little bag (make sure it's closed tight! It helps if you can squeeze out most of the air before sealing) and put the little bag inside the bigger bag filled with ice and salt. Seal up the big bag (tight!). Now, shake the big bag (with the little bag inside it) for 5–7 minutes without stopping. Open the big bag, take out the little bag, and wipe off the outside (of the little bag) with a paper towel to remove the salt water. Open the little bag and enjoy your homemade ice cream. Makes 2 servings.

TO MAKE FLAVORS (ADD BEFORE MIXING):
Cherry vanilla - add chopped maraschino cherries
Strawberry - add ½ cup slightly crushed fresh strawberries
Blueberry - add ½ cup washed, drained fresh blueberries
Chocolate chip - add ½ cup mini chocolate chips
Butterfinger - add 1 tablespoon peanut butter. Do not use vanilla.
    After shaking ice cream, add 2 junior-size crushed Butterfinger
    candy bars before eating
Cookie - add 3 slightly crushed cookies

DAVID BUCK SEALS, REGION 10, TONGASS NATIONAL FOREST, ALASKA

Recipe Index

BREAKFAST

Breakfast Memories 10
Dutch Oven Breakfast 10
Stuffed French Toast 11
Cowboy Breakfast 12
Hungry Man Breakfast...13
Camper's Omelet..14
Sportsman's Breakfast...15
One-Eyed Buffaloes 16
Green River Chile Con Queso Omelet..17
Hunting Camp Scrambled Eggs 18
Hunter's Special Sausage Breakfast Dutch Oven Feast.....................20
Huevos Tixieros 21
River Runnin' Coffee 23
Quick Scones...24

BREADS

Sourdough Bread 27
    About Containers 27
    Making Sourdough Starter...28
    Maintaining Sourdough Starter...29
    Mixing Bread and Biscuits 29
    Sourdough Breads and Biscuits...30
    Dutch Oven and at Home..30
    Sourdough Pancakes 31
Dutch Oven Basque Sheepherder's Bread 32
Sheepherder Bread 33
Dilly Casserole Bread..35
Dutch Oven Beer Bread...36
Spoon Bread 38
Cinnamon Biscuit on a Stick...40
Cinnamon Rolls...41
Breakfast Cinnamon Rolls...42
Heating Tortillas on an Open Fire...44

VEGETABLES

Bert's Dutch Oven Dino Spuds 46
Pan Fried Taters 47
Dutch Oven Potatoes 48
Dutch Oven Spuds and Bacon 49
Grilled Parmesan Potatoes 52
Dutch Oven Spuds 53
Parmesan Mashed Potatoes 54
Dutch Oven Beans 55
Baked Beans 56
Six Bean Casserole 57
Bean Hole Beans 58
Longhorn Beans 59
Basque Green Beans 60
Campsite Lima Beans 61
Onions and Mushrooms 62
Champagne Stuffed Mushrooms 63
Batter Fried Eggplant 65
Grilled Squash 66
Baked Corn, Dutch Oven Style 68

SIDE DISHES

Brown Rice Pilaf 70
Spanish Rice 71
Noodles 73

MAIN DISHES

Spam (Yes, I Said Spam) Casserole 76
Hobo Dinner 77
Flautas 78
Depression Bologna Gravy 80
Chili and Cheese Hot Pot 81
Dutch Oven Quiche 81
Polish Sausage Bake 82
Dutch Oven Stew 84
Son of a Gun Stew 85
Venison Stew 87
Pioneer Night Stew 88
Mile High Stew 89

Moroni Green Chile Stew 90
Boy Scout Stew 91
Beef Stew 92
Paul's Chili 93
Chile Verde Enchiladas 94
Chile Verde 95
Corned Beef and Cabbage 97
Mom's Chili–Souped Up 98
Barbecue Beef and Biscuit Bake 99
Chicken and Noodles 101
Pork and Green Chile Casserole 102
Southwest Chile Roast 103
Dutch Oven One-Pot Meal 106
Fiesta Grilled Ham Steaks 107
Packer John's Super Burger 109
Lasagna Surprise 110
Leonard's Famous Steak Fingers 111
Teriyaki Flank Steak 112
Sweet and Sour Chicken 113
Diamond-X Dutch Oven Hot Wings 114
Dan's Saucy Chicken 116
Grilled Herb Marinated Chicken 117
Zesty Italian Chicken 118
Pistol Rock Chicken 120
Dutch Oven Chicken Marsala 121
Chicken and Salsa Olé 122
Dutch Oven Baked Chicken 123
Beer Roasted Chicken 124
Dutch Oven Parmesan Chicken 125
Sweet and Sour Chicken 127
Potato Chicken Casserole 128
Oven Smoked Turkey 129
Dutch Oven Orange Glazed Stuffed Pork Chops 130
Pork Roast with Black-Eyed Peas 131
Curt's Mouth-Waterin' Barbecue Ribs 132
Never-Fail Pit Barbecue Brisket 136
Salmon Potato Campfire Bake 137
Wilderness Ranger Fish-Cooking Method 138
Dutch Oven Cisco (Bear Lake Cisco) 139
Dutch Oven Seafood Quiche 141

Jack's Beer-Battered Trout (or Halibut, or Any Nice Fish) 142
Great Basin Rattlesnake (Desert Whitefish) 143
Elk Ribs or Brisket Barbecue 144
Barbecue Sauce.. 144
McDuff's Dutch Oven Roast–Venison, Elk, or Moose 145
Shepherd's Pie 146
Baked Dish 147
Hunter's Lunch.. 148
Easy Tamale Pie 149
Sloppy Joe Biscuit Bake 151
Pizza 152
First Night Out Pizza 153
Enchilada Pie 154

DESSERTS

Easy Peach Dutch Oven Cobbler 156
Cherry Cobbler 157
Dutch Oven Cobbler 158
Dutch Oven Fruit Cobbler 159
Caramel Apple Cobbler.. 160
Apple Crunch 162
Mixed Berry Crisp 164
Carrot Pudding 165
Craisin Bread Pudding 166
Piña Colada Cake Dessert 167
Easy Open Fire Cake Dessert.. 168
20-Step Canned Cake 169
Chocolate Lover's Delight 170
Cherry Chocolate Fudge Cake 172
War Cake 174
Canyon Cake 175
Pineapple Upside-Down Cake 176
Coconut Pineapple Cake 177
Coffee Cake 178
Strawberry Shortcake 179
Tasty Campfire Apples in Tinfoil.. 181
Dutch Oven Apple Pie.. 182
Creamy Pumpkin Pie 183
Backpacking Bars 184
Shake and Make Ice Cream 185

Regions of the

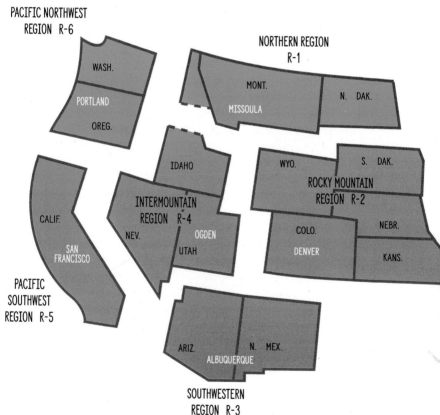

ALASKA
JUNEAU

ALASKA REGION
R-10

PACIFIC NORTHWEST
REGION R-6

WASH.

PORTLAND

OREG.

NORTHERN REGION
R-1

MONT.
MISSOULA

N. DAK.

IDAHO

WYO.

S. DAK.

ROCKY MOUNTAIN
REGION R-2

CALIF.

SAN
FRANCISCO

INTERMOUNTAIN
REGION R-4

NEV.

OGDEN

UTAH

COLO.

DENVER

NEBR.

KANS.

PACIFIC
SOUTHWEST
REGION R-5

ARIZ.

N. MEX.

ALBUQUERQUE

SOUTHWESTERN
REGION R-3

USDA Forest Service

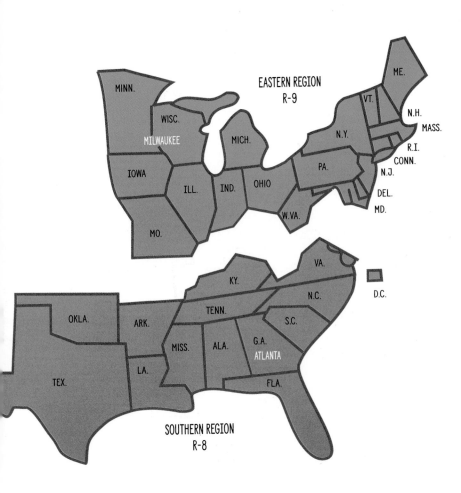

EASTERN REGION
R-9

MINN.

WISC.

MILWAUKEE

MICH.

IOWA

ILL.

IND.

OHIO

W.VA.

MO.

ME.

VT.

N.Y.

N.H.

MASS.

R.I.

CONN.

PA.

N.J.

DEL.

MD.

VA.

KY.

N.C.

D.C.

TENN.

S.C.

OKLA.

ARK.

MISS.

ALA.

G.A.
ATLANTA

TEX.

LA.

FLA.

SOUTHERN REGION
R-8

About the Author

Dedicated volunteers established the National Museum of Forest Service History in Missoula, Montana, in 1988. The Museum is a 501(c)(3) non-profit corporation with the mission to share the rich history and stories of America's conservation legacy.

The organization works to preserve historical objects and documents, develop conservation education, create traveling and virtual exhibits, and will be opening a world-class destination museum in 2025: the National Conservation Legacy Center in Missoula, Montana. Visit forestservicemuseum.org to learn more.

VISIT THE NATIONAL CONSERVATION LEGACY CENTER IN MISSOULA, MONTANA, HOME OF THE NATIONAL MUSEUM OF FOREST SERVICE HISTORY, OPENING 2025.